Courage Through Grace

Change Through Grace

COURAGE
THROUGH
GRACE

A Memoir of War and Peace

Jennie Liston

Xulon Press

Xulon Press
2301 Lucien Way #415
Maitland, FL 32751
407.339.4217
www.xulonpress.com

Unless otherwise indicated, Scripture quotations taken
from the Holy Bible, New International Version (NIV).
Copyright © 1973, 1978, 1984, 2011 by Biblica, Inc.™.
Used by permission. All rights reserved.

Printed in the United States of America.

ISBN-13: 978-1-54566-279-3

Dedication

This book is dedicated posthumously to Jerry, my partner and the love of my life; to my children, Nick and Christine, a constant source of inspiration, pride and blessings; and to my sister Olga, to whom I cling for loving support and companionship.

Acknowledgments

I want to especially thank my patient daughter Christine, who from her familial viewpoint approved and censured content that she felt was uninteresting or superfluous, and who edited the text many times over with her skillful Harvard training to write for critical business executives. Many thanks to my faithful sister Olga, a Princeton graduate, who perused my manuscript for factual accuracy, and corrected flaws that managed to creep in and distort the meaning. Credit and gratitude go to my son Nick, who provided technical support to a completely non-technical parent and put the memoir on the iCloud, saving its contents from a crashed computer.

I am especially indebted to my pastor, Gary Ross, an excellent writer and voluminous reader, who was one of the few readers outside my family to critique my completed manuscript. His enthusiasm—he said he could not put it down once he started reading it and bragged about it to his parish—encouraged me to proceed with its publication.

I want to thank Eve Lebo, my dear friend and colleague, who suggested I take the memoir course and got the memoir started. My instructor Judith Mudd-Krigelmans took it from there and provided inspiration and focus to the content of the memoir, and I'm grateful for her guidance, and for my classmates who reacted so positively to my chapters, read in class.

My other readers and advisors included my sister-in-law Cary, who escaped with the manuscript draft into my bedroom and came out hours later when she had completed reading it. I'm grateful for her enthusiasm and encouragement. My friend Gail Mottola urged me on after reading the first part of the draft and provided valuable insights. I am grateful to her as well.

In writing the memoir, I was once again struck by the marvelous way that God directs a person's life, and His grace in helping to overcome obstacles we might face, so long as our faith in him remains strong. To him be the glory for our successes. I hope my life story will encourage readers to trust God when all else has failed them.

Contents

Introduction

On a cold January morning, as I sit in my favorite easy chair by the fireplace in a lovely house in a small shore town in Delaware, enjoying my morning cup of coffee, I reminisce about my past. My Maltipoo Toby is snoozing quietly on top of the couch next to me, while my adopted cat Cody is stretching luxuriously. After a day of steady rain, the sun is up on this cold winter morning, streaming through the windows and providing a welcome touch to the quiet start of a new day.

Grateful to be alive and relatively healthy in my late seventies, I thank God for the peace I feel as I try to recapture past years and what has brought me to this small shore town at the twilight of my life — a life lived fully. Except for my loyal pets, I am alone in this lovely one-story home — a home that I feel the Lord has given me at this point in my once-hectic life.

My husband of fifty-three years left me at age eighty-two, dying from Parkinson's disease in February of last year. He, and many other military men like him, suffered from Parkinson's for almost ten years, attributed in no small part to his year spent in Viet Nam where he was exposed to Agent Orange. A brilliant scholar who loved people and speaking their languages—he knew six, at least—he was a voracious reader. The sixty boxes of books sitting in my spacious two-car garage attest to that. Jerry, in his last year of suffering with his illness could not speak, read, or write, which was an irony in itself.

It was his struggle with Parkinson's in his last year of life that prompted me to write the memoir. I desperately needed a break from my challenging role of caretaker, and when my friend Eve suggested I take a course in writing memoirs, I signed up for a senior-citizen course held once a week that required a chapter of written content to be produced for reading in class. After struggling with Jerry to get him down at night, I would sit at my desk and work late into the night to prepare for my class the next day. In this way, I produced half the book, and with the encouragement of my instructor and classmates, I proceeded to finish it after the class concluded.

After many years of consulting—primarily for federal agencies that needed to enhance the writing and critical thinking skills of their analysts—I decided to retire and spend my life caring for my wonderful soul mate. It was a job I found more difficult than any I experienced during my lengthy career of almost twenty years as a CIA analyst and a challenging ten years as a traveling consultant thereafter. With the help of my good friends and family, I was able to overcome the challenges of Jerry's difficult final years.

I am content with the decision I made to leave our beloved home in the DC area, where I was surrounded by friends and caring neighbors. Moving to another state where I knew no one was admittedly risky, but it put me closer to my sister who lived in New Jersey and was my eternal friend who was always there when I was in need. My children, although much further away, were within the reach of a phone call, and I knew they would come when needed. Fiercely independent as youngsters, they accepted their mother's need for independence and tolerated her announcements of unexpected actions.

Jerry's funeral in Virginia was memorable and heart wrenching, with his five beloved grandsons and his favorite nephew carrying the casket. The soulful melody of "taps," played perfectly by an army sergeant, brought tears to everyone's eyes. His grandsons and one granddaughter—like his children—doted on Jerry and were proud of his service and loyalty to his country, his knowledge of so many languages, and his awesome football career at the University of Utah, where he played in the East–West game against well-known NFL future "greats," deflecting a final kick to win the game for the West.

We buried Jerry in a lovely cemetery in Millville, New Jersey, next to my parents and brother Nick. It was his wish, despite a plot his parents had for us in Utah. He loved the small Old Orthodox church, where he joined me for its holiday services, and loved speaking Russian to the old bearded men around him. He was one of their own, and they mourned him as he was buried in their cemetery.

It has been a year since his death, and I still miss him terribly, but the wonderful memories I cherish of his love and his patience toward a very impatient wife who made him buy a gold wedding ring at Tiffany's, leave his academic profession for minding a store, and abandon him for two months as she walked the streets of foreign lands, will keep him in my heart until my dying day.

The Lord giveth and He taketh away, I tell myself when loneliness of a single life hits me. But I recover quickly and thank Him for the joys I experienced with a partner who came quietly into my life and left just as peacefully when he took his last breath and looked me straight in the eyes, with open eyes that had been closed for days, as if to say, "Farewell, my love. Until we meet again, be happy."

Close to my new home, the Lewes Ferry sails directly to New Jersey, not far from Millville, where I can visit Jerry, and we can both attest that God's grace is sufficient to get people through anything that life—or death—may bring.

As I look back on our lives, I realize that God's plan for me began while I was still in my mother's womb in a country that was to experience the destruction and violence of the Second World War and the advent of communism, where my story begins.

"And we know that in all things God works for the good of those who love him, who have been called according to his purpose" (Romans 8:28 NIV).

PART ONE

The War Years

Chapter 1

Escape from Latvia and into the War

It was the fall of 1944, and I was five years old. I remember standing on the deck of what I later learned was a German hospital troop ship, gripping the cold steel handrail and trying to figure out what was happening on the sidewalk below. My dad was gesturing in excitement to Grandad, telling him something emphatically, while Mom stood holding Grandma's hands. I remember Grandma's long black coat and a black scarf framing her kind, round face, from which tears were flowing steadily. This upset me, especially since Mom was also crying. Both women were crying and hugging each other.

My brother Nick was next to me, and I could tell he was confused. I stepped closer to him and took his cold hand in mine, trying to comfort him. Although my brother was a year older, I felt like I was the mature one at that moment. I was as confused as he was, but I knew that whatever was happening could not be good.

We were all supposed to board the ship and go for a visit to Germany, according to our folks, but the scene below told me, even at five years of age, that this was not going to be a happy visit.

Suddenly, my grandmother fell over against my mom, who tried desperately to hold her up. Dad and Grandad rushed over to her and helped to support her. I wanted to run down as well and started forward, but something held me back and I knew that we had to stay put. I was right. Dad looked up at us and yelled for us to stay where we were. Dad's warning made me realize that this was not going to be an adventure, as Mom had promised, and I suspected correctly that Grandma and Grandpa would not be going with us, as we were told earlier.

The ship's loud horn of warning that it was about to depart startled me and seemed to wake up my grandmother, who tried to stand and move into Mom's arms, while leaning on Grandad's shoulder. They continued to talk, making me nervous that our parents would also miss our departure and leave us standing alone as the ship sailed away. I guess Dad must have realized that this could happen because he hugged his parents for the last time and propelled Mom by the shoulders toward the ship, leaving our grandparents behind, waving on the sidewalk.

Mom and Dad rushed up the plank and stood next to us, as the ship began to leave the port, waving to our grandparents as they stood there, becoming smaller as we moved away. Mom turned to Dad and gripped his hand tightly. "I'm so relieved that you made it here in time," she said softly to Dad. "Was it hard for you to get away?"

"It certainly wasn't easy, and I was lucky to make it in time," he said with a sigh, and proceeded to tell Mom about his recent effort to get away from his office and meet us here at the ship.

Leaving Latvia in the fall of 1944 was almost impossible, since the communists were quickly closing off all exits to the outside world. To make matters worse, the Bolsheviks began to suspect my dad's motives and watched his every step, detailing a militiaman to guard him at work and to see him home at night. Dad worked late and had little time for us, coming home exhausted, but he found an opportunity to move the family out of our stately two-story brick house in Riga and to send us to stay with his parents in Daugavpils, a city on the border of Latvia and Poland, where he thought we might be safer.

Within a week, Dad learned that a German hospital ship was coming to take wounded Germans back to Germany and, with his knowledge of German and some gold coins, was able to arrange passage for us all on the ship in return for helping with care of the wounded. He even got them to agree that he could bring his mom and dad with us.

"It's such a shame that they decided to stay in Latvia at the last moment," he said to Mom, as he watched them disappear in the distance. "We'll probably never see them again."

"But how did you manage to escape from your job, and were you able to stop at the house?" Mom wanted to know.

Dad proceeded to describe his daring escape from work, when he bribed the guard, who was his watchdog, and quickly fled to our house located in the heart of Riga not far from his office. There he took the few items that he had packed earlier, including a family icon of the Holy Mother of God, whom he considered his protectorate.

While Dad was gathering his things and taking a last look at the lovely home we had lived in for six years, he heard noises outside and saw a group of militiamen approaching the front door. Running to the basement, he quickly climbed out of the cold storage door behind the house and ran for the woods that surrounded the spacious brick home. He heard shots behind him as he darted into the woods and hid in some thick shrubs where he could see the house and the men scurrying around it.

No one had followed him to the woods, as it appeared the men had other business. They were lighting torches and throwing them in the windows of the house. Dad watched in horror as the house that held such pleasant memories of his quieter life was set on fire, distressed to see it burn with all its precious contents.

"I was unable to stop the destruction," he told Mom, who was holding her head in shock, "so I said a quick prayer, and proceeded to the port to meet you all, as we had arranged."

I did not want to hear that we no longer had a home to go back to and closed my eyes to shut out the image of our lovely house burning to the ground. I could see my favorite dolls, especially Dusya, squirming horribly in the heat and then burning into a charred black stick. The thought of it made me want to cry, and I choked back a sob that was loud enough to make Mom hug me and gently direct me downstairs where we would be staying during the journey out of Latvia and to Germany.

As Mom made us comfortable in the hold of the ship and slipped a blanket around my shoulders, I sat on the floor and started to cry silently as I thought of losing our house and my grandparents all at once. I loved both the house and my grandparents who I wanted to join us on our trip. They were kind and loving. They seldom scolded us, allowing us to run around freely on their large country farm. Even when we disobeyed them and got too close to the geese that waddled around in the yard and came after us with a vengeance on one of our visits, we were not reprimanded. Grandpa saved us from being painfully pecked by putting his body between them and us as we ran screeching to the house.

7

He was silent as he cleaned the blood from his hands with his yellowing handkerchief. The sight of the blood, he figured, was a good lesson to us for the future. He was right; we never came close to the geese again.

We had fun staying with them when my parents took a train trip to get away or visit relatives in St. Petersburg, Russia. To be honest, Nick was the one who stayed with them the most lately. My parents felt that we needed to be divided between both sets of grandparents, and I usually got to stay with my maternal grandmother. She was a stern disciplinarian, and Nick often misbehaved when he was with her and then got reprimanded. He always put up a fuss when he thought he was going to her house, so my parents ended up sending me there.

I didn't mind. I found my maternal grandmother Katya to be a fascinating person and got along well with her. She took me around her large estate, introduced me to her help, who showed me how they milked the cows and let me taste the warm, rich milk they produced. I loved to watch them groom the horses and occasionally got a ride on the slower ones. Grandma Katya also taught me how to recognize good mushrooms from poisonous ones during our walks in the woods, as I helped her pick them for meals.

My paternal grandfather was never around, and when I asked Grandma Katya about him, she told me that he was away at war. I later learned that Granddad was a decorated general in the White Russian Army and fought at the front against the Bolsheviks. He left Grandma early in their marriage, after a dispute they had about his refusal to work on the estate. He was, after all, a son of nobility and preferred to spend his day riding, playing with Mom, his small daughter, and meeting with friends to drink and play cards.

His ultimate fate was unknown, but when my parents were about to be married, Mom heard that he was somewhere in the area and asked Grandma if they could send word to him to attend the wedding. Grandma wouldn't hear of this and vehemently opposed it, insisting that their lives would be at risk if he ever showed up.

The battles between the White Russians and Bolsheviks were fierce, and the Whites lost many of their soldiers, leaving them and their families at great risk of being annihilated. Grandma and her family had taken great care to burn all documents connected to Grandpa, and their name had been changed to reflect Grandma Katya's first marriage to a landowner twice her age who died of some unknown disease, leaving his young wife with three children to run his large estate.

Grandma Katya had met her second husband while visiting her sister in St. Petersburg and fell in love with the dashing young officer. Mom was the product of their union, but she had two older stepsisters and one older stepbrother who was like a father to her. Grandpa had threatened to take his daughter Verochka with him when he left. Grandma Katya knew he was serious and hid my mom in one of her estates in Poland that Grandpa didn't know about, staying there until Grandpa got tired of searching for them. Mom was very young at the time, and she could not even remember what her father looked like. She had no idea what his real name was when I asked her about him.

I had been hoping that this trip to Germany would be a chance for me to enjoy both my grandparents again, but Dad made it clear that Grandma Katya was not interested in the trip to Germany; she had too many responsibilities at home. And here we were, losing the company of our paternal grandparents as well.

We left Latvia in 1944, toward the end of the Second World War. The Allies were bombing Germany from all directions, so we literally went from the frying pan into the fire. The Baltic country of Latvia, which had enjoyed a short period as an independent country, was invaded first by the Germans and then the Bolsheviks, who chased them out and began to take over the port city of Riga, where my father worked as the country's administrator of railroads. Because he kept the railroads running smoothly despite the upheaval, the Bolsheviks kept him alive, in contrast to his brother-in-law and many other city leaders, who were taken from their homes and were never seen again, while their wives and children were moved out of Latvia to Siberia.

Chapter 2

A Precarious Journey

I had never been on a ship before, and the hustle and bustle of men running around and shouting orders in a strange language, carrying wounded soldiers below deck, and manning the large guns on deck fascinated me enough to keep me from feeling frightened and out of place. We were not the only refugees to leave Latvia, and we were directed to go below deck with other women and children whose husbands worked on the opposite side of the ship. Nick and I clung to our mother, who ushered us toward a corner and sat us down on the ship's dirty floor, wrapping a warm blanket around us.

The sound of the ship's motors that had frightened me at first became a lulling backdrop, as I closed my eyes and rested against Mom's warm body. I was surprised at how tired I was, but it had been a long day of traveling by train from Daugavpils with our grandparents, and the trauma of leaving them behind was still fresh in my mind. I wanted to shut the scene out of my memory, and before long I was asleep and dreaming of being reunited with my grandmother—and coming home with her to our beloved Riga house with the large fountain surrounded by a circular driveway in the front yard welcoming us.

I don't know how long I slept, but a loud "boom" suddenly pierced the silence, making me sit straight up next to Mom, and I felt fear gripping me as more shots rang out. The ship felt like it was swaying precariously, and I grabbed my mother's hand, unable to comprehend what was going on. Nick began to cry, and Mom pulled both of us to her bosom, shushing us as she prayed in a loud whisper. I could feel her body trembling, and I held on for dear life.

After what seemed like hours, the firing stopped and the ship, which had been swaying wildly, steadied and began to rock gently, as it had before. I heard a woman who sat across from us saying loudly, "I think I heard planes overhead; they must have tried to sink us."

"Yes," my mother replied, "but God saved us from the attack." It was a long time before I could fall asleep again, waiting for another attack to come at any time. As I finally drifted off, I heard my dad's voice comforting my mother.

"The Germans must have mistaken us for a Russian vessel, until the crew was able to hoist a German flag for them to see that it was a German hospital ship," he explained. "The ship will dock in Bremerhaven," he added, "and we'll see if we can get to Bremen and then to Hamburg from there."

"Why are we going to Bremen?" I asked sleepily.

"They have a good railroad system that can get us to Hamburg and from there, we will try to get to Denmark, where it should be safe," he explained. "Denmark is neutral, so we can get away from the bombing there."

"Are we going to be bombed again?" I asked fearfully.

"Hopefully we can escape north and get away from the war," Dad said.

We arrived in Bremerhaven as the day dawned, and I again heard men running up and down the metal stairs of the ship. One tall German in uniform with shiny boots came to our cabin and propelled us up the stairs to the deck, where we met up with Dad. They unloaded us and our small pieces of luggage, boarding us on army trucks that took us to a large empty warehouse in the middle of a clearing. There they separated the men from the women and children, and took us to one corner of the warehouse, while they forced the men to stay outside.

They made us all sit on the sandy floor of the ware-house amid large wooden boxes and wait for further orders. I noticed that Mom seemed tense and appeared frightened, while some of the other women were crying softly. "Mom, what's happening now?" I whispered to her.

"It's all right; just stay quiet," she replied in a whisper. Soon, several uniformed men appeared and started to separate the mothers from their children. As they approached my mother, Nick and I moved closer to her, clutching her arms. A German soldier grabbed us both roughly and jerked us away from Mom, plopping us on the dirty floor. We both began to cry loudly, as Mom strained toward us.

Just then, the door flew open to our room and two officers rushed in, barking orders to the soldiers who had been pushing us around. They proceeded to usher them out, leaving us alone. I could hear the sighs of relief from the women in the room. Mom quickly picked us up from the floor, dusted us off, and said a quick prayer of thanks before Dad appeared at the door with the other husbands, who began to comfort their wives and children. Dad told us that we were safe, but at the time I did not understand that Mom and the other women were spared from rape by the soldiers, who were notorious for violating their captives, even in front of their children.

With Germany at risk from increased Allied bombing, the soldiers had to leave for their unit and return to the war front, while we needed to move out to find our way to Hamburg, which Dad had learned had a large refugee camp.

Chapter 3

Racing My Brother to the Safety of Shelters

When we finally arrived at the refugee camp in Hamburg that my father had heard about, the Germans took us to a series of army barracks that stood just outside the city of Hamburg and led us into one that was to be our home for the next few weeks. The barracks were all crowded with refugees from a variety of former Soviet Union countries, all trying to escape the onslaught of communism; ours held refugees from the Baltic countries of Latvia, Estonia, and Lithuania, prime targets for the Soviets because of their access to the Baltic Sea and Europe.

Our little space consisted of two bunk beds, several chairs, a table, and material curtain-like dividers that separated us from our immediate neighbors. Privacy was almost nonexistent since neighbors heard every word uttered. Dad slept with my brother Nick in the top bunk, and Mom slept with me in the bottom one. Common bathrooms had to accommodate at least twenty people, including children. Another area of barracks was designated for the kitchen and dining room where all were fed rather meager portions and selection.

As a youngster of five, I did not miss my privacy except when my parents shushed me as I complained about something others should not hear. One of my main complaints was the lack of space for us and other children to run around in. Nick and I got tired of sitting on our bunks and were running out of games to play. Dad patted my head gently and promised to do his best to get us some fresh air.

The window we shared with neighbors was opened occasionally to air out the room, and I loved crouching by it to smell the fresh outside air, even when it was filled with smells of fried food being prepared in the cafeteria. I was always hungry since we were limited in what and how much we could eat. As the bombing became more pronounced, that window was kept open, so the elderly folks who were left to tend the children could throw us outside quickly to run to the shelters. The Germans began to increasingly use the refugee adult population to run their factories, especially as many Germans left town for safer places. During the day, as a result, children were the responsibility of elderly folks and an occasional German nursemaid.

The one time we were given the opportunity to wander outside was when a big German woman trained us to run to shelters if we should hear the sirens and the area was at risk of being bombed. To this day, I shudder when I remember the shrill sirens that sent us running toward these underground shelters as we were thrown out of our windows and told to run quickly to the shelters about a half block away.

My brother Nick was probably the fastest kid on the block. His long legs moved like two motorcycle wheels, and he always arrived at the shelters ahead of me, which made me cry and slowed my progress. Once I got there, I always had trouble finding him in the crush of sweaty bodies packed into a small space, including the Germans who remained in the barracks and the older folks who watched over us. I can still remember the feeling of being all alone, separated from loved ones and squeezed between numerous frightened humans. I yearned for the warm body of my mom or the solid bulk of my dad at times like those.

After we had been in the barracks in Hamburg for several weeks, my father announced quietly one day that we were going to leave as soon as possible. "I heard the Germans saying at the factory that they were expecting a large attack from the Allies in the next few days," he told Mom.

"But how can we do that?" she asked. "You know they have posted a guard at the outside door at night, and he lets no one out."

"I'll find a way," Dad promised.

With his knowledge of railroads and how they functioned, Dad learned that a train with open boxcars of coal was the only train leaving Hamburg in the following week. Two days before it was to depart, Dad reconnoitered the area to find an empty boxcar where we could hide out until time for the train to leave. He planned to take us there that night, having bribed the camp guard to allow us to leave the camp.

I remember getting a knapsack to put my precious belongings in, as well as some canned goods and crackers, taken from the cafeteria that day. As we waited for night to fall, Dad gave us strict directions on what we were to do when we left the barracks. "I want both of you to be as quiet as you can when it's time for us to walk to the outside door. Just follow me—Mom will be behind you. Don't say a word and walk as quietly as you can."

In the middle of the night, Mom woke us up, and Dad led us to the door of the barracks, expecting to see the familiar guard whom he had bribed. Instead, we found a sour-faced alternate who barked at us in German and, at gunpoint, told us all to return to our rooms, threatening to jail us if we tried it again. I cried on and off all day after my parents left for work the next morning, feeling the weight of the world on my shoulders and thinking that we would all be blown up by the bombs, which were sure to come if we did not get away.

Despite our first unsuccessful attempt to leave the barracks, Dad told us that we would try it again the following night, in case the bribed guard was on duty. "I'm afraid," I wailed. "What if the guard decides to shoot us this time?"

"We're in God's hands," Dad said confidently. "Either way, we will be fine. Just trust Him and do what I tell you to do tonight."

Our second attempt to escape met with success. The guard whom Dad bribed appeared again and allowed us to escape, and we quietly followed Dad outside.

The cold air outside took my breath away but was a welcome change from the stifling heat in the barracks. I felt free as we walked down the quiet German streets to our destination and tried to ignore the hunger pangs in my stomach. I had eaten very little that evening, maybe out of nervousness and because I was trying to save the meager portions to put in my backpack that night.

We approached the railroad and walked along the tracks as Dad instructed, arriving at a series of boxcars standing on the tracks. Dad slid back the door of a large black boxcar, and it squeaked loudly as he pulled it back. Once inside, I was shocked to see that it looked occupied, as Dad lit a candle to give us some light. In the center, stood a crate that resembled a table and on it was a large pot filled with, of all things, a split pea soup with a ham bone. Under the pot stood a pan that had held hot coals, still simmering and giving off some heat to keep the soup warm. "Dad, how did this get here? Can we eat the soup?" Nick and I asked hesitantly.

"Of course," he replied. "I befriended some kind Germans who promised to feed us before we left the city. Looks like they outdid themselves."

Dad was my hero, and I believed he could do anything, but this was even more than I expected. He had a way of making friends with almost anyone he met, and his resourcefulness kept us alive and together during the chaotic times of the war. His knowledge of German and ability to speak like a native helped to impress the Germans, who were willing to accommodate him and his needs. He reciprocated by rewarding them generously with cigarette cartons he earned but, as a nonsmoker, was always ready to give away, a rarity much coveted during the war years and after.

To this day, split pea soup is my favorite, and when I eat it, I think of how delicious it tasted that night. Having filled our empty stomachs, my brother and I soon drifted off to sleep, with the assurance that Mom would wake us up when it was time to leave. Departure came much quicker than we would have liked. Mom's gentle hand on my cheek woke me up reluctantly, and we dressed quietly, gathering our meager belongings, and walked out into the moon-lit frosty night.

Once outside the friendly boxcar, Dad led us to a train standing on the tracks with open boxcars stretching into the distance. After walking past what seemed like a dozen cars, Dad stopped us and climbed up one open car, looked inside, and climbed back half way, motioning to Mom to help us climb to meet him. He lifted us into the coal car and settled us all down on top of the coals, where a tarp covered the sharp edges of the contents. He took another tarp from the far side of the car and covered us with it, leaving one side open for us to look out. We lay there quietly, at first feeling uncomfortable but then got used to the hardness of the coal under our bodies.

Dad was asleep in no time at all, while the rest of us gazed at the open sky in anticipation. He had been up several nights in a row, and exhaustion finally hit him. "Let's say our prayers," Mom suggested, and both Nick and I recited our evening prayers. The prayers calmed me, and I was soon asleep but awoke several times in discomfort. Nick did the same, and only Mom stayed awake, too nervous to go to sleep. At one time I heard her waking Dad in fear, as she saw planes flying overhead. "Volodya, wake up. I think we are going to be bombed, and the train is not moving at all."

"Relax, Vera! We are in God's hands now, and we just need to trust Him for our safety," he replied, going back to sleep.

I don't know when it happened, but I felt the train surge to a start and slowly pull out of the station, picking up speed as it went. The engineer was undoubtedly as anxious to leave as we were. We left Hamburg, just as the city experienced one of the worst bombings in the war and was completely devastated.

Chapter 4

Running from the War

We got away from Hamburg, but the coal car took us south to Leipzig, another town engulfed in bombing and destruction, and not north where my father hoped it would take us. He was aiming our path toward Denmark, a neutral state and one he felt would be safe for the family.

The train, which had gathered steam as it left Hamburg, continued at its break-neck speed, failing to stop in any nearby town. Once it reached Leipzig, it screeched to a stop, and the train uncoupled from its coal cars. We were all sore from the uncomfortable positions on top of the coal as well as dirty from its black contents. Having spent a night and a day, huddling for warmth on the open flat car, we were more than ready to leave.

"Where are we?" I asked Dad as he lowered us to the ground. "Are we where you were planning to take us in Germany?" I asked hopefully.

"No, honey," he replied sadly. "It took us south instead of north, so we still have quite a distance to go." I felt tired and disappointed, and all I could think of was a clean bed and some good food. My stomach was growling, and the memory of the split pea soup intruded on my thoughts.

"When can we eat, Dad?" Nick asked before I could do so, and I waited for Dad's answer.

"It might be some time, Nick," Dad responded. "Eat some of the crackers you have in your knapsack, as I look for another train that can take us out of here."

"Volodya," my mom interjected. "Wasn't it somewhere around Leipzig that your brother and his family were settled? I remember the letter he sent you to Latvia about a half year ago, urging you to move the family out of Riga and bring them to Germany. Of course, things have changed with all the bombing, but he mentioned living in the country near Leipzig. Do you have his address with you?"

"You are right, Verochka," Dad said, as his voice sounded hopeful. "And I do have his address, of course. Let's see if I can find it quickly," Dad said as he took out his address book. Looking at the book, he frowned and told us, "I'm afraid Vitaliy and his family are closer to Berlin, which is north of Leipzig. Let's see if we can find a train to take us in that direction."

We started into the main train station, and I was shocked to see it overcrowded with refugees everywhere, trying to find their way to a departing train. "What's going on?" Dad asked a German. "Why is the station so packed with people?"

"Word is," the man responded, "the bombs are coming to Leipzig tonight, and everyone is trying to get out of the city, but very few trains are moving out. We are waiting for a train to come shortly, so we can catch it to Berlin, but the mob of people makes it almost impossible to get close to the tracks," the German confided.

"Let's get in line," Dad told us, as we approached the railroad track that the German had pointed to. Men, women, and children were packed in like sardines, and we had to push like the others to move closer to the track. Dad and Mom held us closely, as we heard the sound of a train whistle in the distance. The crowd in front of the tracks was being pushed closer to the edge, and Dad moved us away from it, as if sensing the danger of being pushed onto the tracks below.

I saw the locomotive appear in the distance and felt the panic of the crowd as everyone tried to get closer to the tracks in order to board first. To my horror, the people in front were being pushed onto the tracks, right in front of the oncoming train. I closed my eyes and could not watch to see what happened as the train approached, fearing it could not stop. My worst fears were realized, as the train continued to come, unable to stop in time to avoid those unlucky ones being thrown in front of it. I heard screeching of the wheels as the conductor tried to stop the moving train and avoid hitting at least a dozen women, men, and children who had fallen on the tracks. "Help them," I heard myself shout, squinting through half-closed eyes, afraid to open them completely.

Dad and Mom quickly moved us away from the bedlam that ensued, with people crying and trying to get to their loved ones now lying under the wheels of the train. I sobbed loudly as we walked away from the front of the train, being herded by Dad and pushed by the crowd to the cars in the back. The scene was so horrifying that I had nightmares for many years afterward, as my dreams replayed the train hitting its helpless passengers-to-be. I felt like I was falling in front of it as well.

We waited to board the train until they cleared out the dead and injured. Suddenly I felt my dad lifting me and shoving me through a window in one of the back cars of the train, with Nick following after me. People inside helped us to a seat, and we anxiously waited for our parents to arrive.

With the crowds so dense, passengers trying to board were putting their children in through the open windows and then shoving their way to the doors of the cars where the children were deposited. I later learned that many families were separated in this way, when parents could not make it through the train doors before the train pulled away. Fortunately, we were not among them, as Dad and Mom appeared after what seemed like a very long time, and sat down beside us. Dad had apparently run several cars down with Mom and proceeded to board where it was less crowded and then walked through the train cars until they found us.

As the train pulled away, packed to its capacity, we all breathed a sigh of relief. "Where is it going?" I heard Mom ask Dad.

"I really don't know, but it should stop along the way once it clears Leipzig, and we'll get out to look for my brother Vitaliy and his family. It appears to be going in the right direction, to Berlin, and we can figure out how to get to their village as we get closer and at a safe distance from Leipzig."

Chapter 5

Family Reunion: Comfort and a Breath of Fresh Air

T he train to Berlin made a number of stops along the way, and although it was packed and we had to sit on our parents' laps most of the way, it was a welcome change from the coal car. As we approached Berlin, Dad announced that we would disembark shortly if the train should stop. "What is the town we're stopping in?" I asked Dad. "Are Uncle Vitaliy and his family living there?"

"Yes," Dad told us. "It's a small town called Potsdain, not far from Berlin. Last time he wrote us, he gave me the address, and I think we can find it with the help of the local Germans."

The train stopped for a short time, and we all got off, happy to be able to walk in the fresh air. Potsdain was a lovely town, surrounded by lush farmland and showing no signs of bombing or destroyed homes. Dad soon had us walking down a narrow cobblestone street, looking for the address of our Uncle Vitaliy and his family. After several stops to question Germans on the directions, we arrived at a large farm with a stately manor house and a number of small huts that held the farm workers and their families. Uncle Vitaliy and his wife Aunt Fanya came running to us as Dad knocked on the door of a slightly larger house as compared to the small huts around it.

It was late afternoon, and the sun was already setting, the air was fresh and it actually felt warm, given the late October date. I was exhilarated. After getting a hug from Aunt Fanya, I started to skip and run around her and Uncle Vitaliy as they hugged Mom and Dad and stood quietly talking. "Volodya," my uncle—who looked so much like my Dad, only taller—said "how in the world did you get here? I'm so glad to see you are all safe and sound."

"Thanks to God, Vitya," Dad responded, and proceeded to tell him how we managed to leave Latvia. "You were smart to get out early," Dad told his brother. "Our sister and her family were not as lucky."

Dad's brother-in-law was killed by the Bolsheviks, and Aunt Manya and the three children were sent to Siberia. Dad discovered in horror that the Bolsheviks had awakened her and her three children at night, and still in their night clothes, including the eight-month old baby, had loaded them into an empty boxcar without food or water. Dad stumbled on them when he was alerted by his staff to check what were supposed to be empty boxcars being moved to Siberia but were used for the inhumane treatment of our families by the Bolsheviks.

"Was there anything you could do to get them out?" Aunt Fanya asked incredulously.

"Short of being killed on the spot, I had no power to free them," Dad responded in agony. "They had guards with rifles standing by each boxcar."

After making sure they were fine, Dad quickly got Mom, and they both brought them warm clothes, food, and water. He also made the soldiers put water in all the boxcars filled with people, despite the risk to do so. The next day, he was questioned about his behavior and angrily told the Bolshevik confronting him what he thought of their inhumane treatment of the city's foremost leaders and their families.

"Boy, you sure were taking a chance there," said Uncle Vitaliy. "You were probably on their list next, after our brother-in-law, the mayor, and city administrator."

"Comrade," the Bolshevik had shouted at Dad, "you are lucky that you and your family have been spared, despite being enemies of the state, and only because you are indispensable."

Dad said this made him realize that it was only a matter of time before we would all be at risk and was determined to get us out of Latvia as soon as possible.

"I learned that a German hospital ship was coming to take wounded Germans back to Germany and was able to arrange passage for us all on the ship, in return for helping with care of the wounded. I even got them to agree that I could bring Mom and Dad with us," he told Uncle Vitya. "But unfortunately they decided to stay in Latvia at the last moment, just as we were getting ready to board the ship."

"What a shame," said Uncle Vitaliy sadly. "We'll probably never see them again."

"How did you get away? Weren't they watching you closely?" asked Aunt Fanya.

"They certainly were. My challenge was to escape unnoticed on the day of departure. I had asked our dad to bring the family to the port from Daugavpils on that day. He and Mom had the kids and Vera, whom I had taken there earlier."

"Let's go inside," Aunt Fanya interrupted, as she looked at our tired faces. "You must be exhausted and hungry," she added.

The little house was simply furnished but clean and inviting. It had two small bedrooms and a small kitchen, but a good-sized living area with a fireplace. Uncle Vitaliy was the farm's horticulturalist and landscape architect and was paid well by the wealthy Germans living in the large manor house. His trade and the way he kept the farm and gardens fruitful with his green thumb earned him the use of the house and its furnishings, as well as a decent salary to keep them all living modestly.

Aunt Fanya had just baked some fresh bread, and the smell of it permeated the entire house. Nick and I looked hungrily at it, and Aunt Fanya immediately cut fresh pieces of it, buttered it generously, and handed it to us. We both devoured the large piece she gave each of us and licked our lips like cats after a fresh bowl of milk.

As we settled down on the couch, the door opened, and our two cousins, Vasiliy and Boris came walking in. Vasiliy was the elder, at that time around fourteen years old, and Boris was seven, slightly older than Nick. They had done some work on the farm after coming home from school. They greeted us warmly, and we all proceeded to talk, with Nick and me giving them the highlights of our life in Germany after leaving Latvia. Following a delicious dinner of bratwurst, cabbage, and potatoes, we settled on a pillow near the fireplace and listened to the adults talking.

"I want to know how you were able to escape the communists who needed your services," said Uncle Vitaliy to Dad. "Weren't they making sure that you came to work daily?" As tired as I was, Dad's story kept me awake until he finished telling it.

I did not want to hear that we no longer had a home to go back to and closed my eyes to shut out the image of our lovely house burning to the ground. The thought of it made me want to cry, and I choked back a sob that was loud enough to make the adults turn toward me and my mother move to comfort me. She covered me with a

32

warm blanket and rubbed my head gently until I felt my eyes close. Exhaustion hit me, and I fell sound asleep on the floor near the fireplace, despite some animated discussions going on around me.

We did not stay long with our uncle and aunt. There really was not enough room for all of us in the house, and Dad had already decided that he wanted to take us to Denmark, away from the bombs and the destruction that was sure to come to this idyllic little village as well. After visiting for several days, we prepared to depart, and Uncle Vitaliy took us to the railroad from which we had arrived.

When the war ended, Uncle Vitaliy and his family had an opportunity to settle in Australia, which was accepting refugees from the Baltics. They tried to find out how our relatives were faring behind the Iron Curtain in Latvia and were able to contact them by mail. The response that came from our grandfather was a chilling one. Grandpa told them that they should most certainly return to Daugavpils, where they could celebrate together with family members who my uncle knew had been killed and buried before and during the war. "Don't even try to return" was the hidden message.

Since a return to Latvia was closed to them, my uncle and his family moved to Melbourne, Australia, where they remained the rest of their lives, except for a trip my uncle made to visit us shortly before his death. Dad, who carefully avoided flying in an airplane, took a flight to Los Angeles, where my uncle had to change planes, to escort his brother to New Jersey, and accompanied him back there to see him safely board the return flight to Australia before returning home.

Chapter 6

War Comes to an End

I did not realize what a breath of fresh air it was to visit with Uncle Vitya and Aunt Fanya until we were on the road again. Our next stop was in Berlin, where Dad was able to find a boarding house and a room in which we could spend a week until he figured out how to get to Denmark safely. Berlin had been bombed soundly and was always under threat of more bombing. Dad found the nearest shelter for us to escape to when the sirens sounded, and our first night there gave us good practice to outrun the bombs. I was awakened by the sound of sirens and frightened enough to get dressed quickly and follow Mom and Dad to the shelter. This time, I did not have to race with Nick but felt fortunate to have Dad usher us out of the house and to the nearby shelter. Fortunately, the bombs did not destroy the house we were staying in, and we were able to return there after several hours of clinging to each other for warmth and safety.

The next night we were all sound asleep when a loud bang and the sound of glass breaking woke us up suddenly. "Volodya," I heard my mom asking fearfully. "What was that?"

"I don't know," he replied. "It sounded like a rock hitting our window. I'll take a look," he said, and climbed out of the bed next to us.

"It is a rock, and a large one at that," he told us, after examining the floor. "I'm afraid the window is shattered. We were blessed not to be near the window or where it fell," he added, examining the large, round rock lying on the floor in the middle of the room.

We all heard loud voices and laughter outside, but Dad told us to stay away from the window. "Sounds like some German hoods are trying to send us a message," he said. "I heard they did not like refugees cluttering up their country," he explained. "I'll try to get us out of here as soon as I can buy some tickets to Hamburg."

Hamburg, I thought. I did not want to go back there, as I remembered the crowded refugee camp, running to shelters, and watching in horror as people were pushed in front of the train at the train station.

"Dad," I asked sleepily. "Why do we have to go back there? I don't like that place."

"We have very little choice. The train to Hamburg is also the one we need to get to Denmark. The coal car took us out of our way south, and we need to go back north to get to where it's safe."

I knew that Dad would figure it all out, but I was certainly not looking forward to going back to Hamburg. I snuggled under the covers and prayed that we would have a safe journey to Denmark in spite of the war and the threat of being bombed.

The train to Hamburg was like the rest—crowded, smelling of people's sweat and babies' diapers, and stopping along the way in every town, slowing our progress to Denmark. From Hamburg, we took another train to Flensburg, on the border of Germany and Denmark. In Flensburg, Dad learned that refugees were not allowed to cross the border to Denmark, a shock and disappointment to all of us, and proceeded to find a refugee camp for us to stay in. While it was similar to the other refugee camps we stayed in along the way, it was not as crowded, and we actually had a small apartment of our own. Flensburg was also out of the way of the bombs, and we spent some restful days and nights there, without the screeching sound of sirens that we had gotten used to in our journey north.

World War II came to an end while we were in Flensburg. I remember only too well seeing refugees hug each other and jump for joy at the prospect of peace finally coming. The city had a large celebration in the streets at night, with music, good food, and dancing in the streets. I decided that I might like this town after all and was especially happy to see my parents smiling and laughing, something I had missed during our travels in Germany.

Dad soon found a job in Flensburg, and we moved to a nice apartment on the second story of a large house. We settled in comfortably, enjoying a much quieter life after the horrors of the war, thinking we would live there forever. My little sister Olga was born in Flensburg, and I remember how Nick and I wrote letters to Mom in the hospital, telling her that Dad had made yogurt for us and built us little skis to walk in the snow and ski down the gentle slopes of Flensburg's small hills. I still have the child-like letters we wrote to Mom in Latvian. Life was good in Flensburg, and I was disappointed to hear several years later that Dad received an invitation for the family to live in a country called America.

"Let's not go," I told Mom. "It's fun here, and I don't want to travel across an ocean to a country far away. What if we don't like it there?" I was nine years old at the time and had developed a large group of friends during our three years of living there. The idea of leaving them did not appeal to me.

PART TWO

Life in America

Chapter 7

Lady Liberty Calls for a New Way of Life

I t was the spring of 1949, and we were on a ship again — *The Marina Marlene* — heading for America. This was a large ship, compared to the one we took from Latvia in 1944, churning across the Atlantic Ocean to the United States of America.

I remember very little about the voyage, except for the pitching and tossing of the ship and how seasick we all were. My mother, my three-year-old sister Olga, and I were housed in the lower deck with other women; the men were in a different part of the ship. Dad and Nick came to visit us on calmer days, since they, too, suffered from seasickness. I spent a lot of time in bed, trying to get over the queasy feeling that never seemed to leave me, and swore that I would never take another ship ride to anywhere. It was a long ten-day journey, which seemed to have no end, but finally, when I thought I could not take it for one more day, Dad came to tell us that we were about to land. Excitement seemed to mount as we approached Ellis Island. It looked like the entire population of the ship appeared on the upper deck to get a sight of Lady Liberty through the thick fog. I heard chatter all around me, and a lot of prayers that we had arrived safely to America. I was soon caught up in the anticipation of a new life in a new country—a country that everyone talked about with awe in their voices.

My parents had decided, after a lot of prayer, that God wanted them in America rather than Germany, and that He had specific plans for us all. My dad had been sponsored as a potential priest for the Old Orthodox Church in Millville, New Jersey, where a sizeable group of Russian Old Orthodox (or Old Believers, as they were called) had settled in the 1930s, built a church, and were served by a priest who was approaching his 90s. The Old Believers were part of a large group of Orthodox Christians who split from the Russian Orthodox Church in the 1600s and were persecuted in Russia for not adhering to the changes that were brought into the Orthodox Church by Archpriest Nicon. To stay alive, these Old Believers had to scatter to all parts of the world, with some ending up in China, Turkey, Alaska, Siberia, and closer to Russia, in Poland and Belarus, as well as the Baltics, where my ancestors ended up in Latvia.

Dad was an Old Orthodox seminarian, as well as an engineer by training, to the extent that the Old Orthodox had a seminary in Latvia. Mainly, it was a study of the Old Orthodox liturgy, its ancient way of reading music and singing—by hooks rather than notes—and knowledge of the order of service on Sundays and holidays, and the rites of the Old Orthodox faith. This was learned in classes in the evenings and during the services, which were numerous.

A faithful churchgoer in his youth, Dad became even more involved as an adult, despite his demanding job, seldom missing a church service. He had a wonderful tenor voice, which he used to lead the church choir, since the services did not allow any instruments, and the singing was a capella. His reputation as a valuable and faithful church attendee spread through the large Riga Old Orthodox community, so when some of the Old Orthodox members came to America as refugees from the Second World War and were sponsored by the Millville Old Orthodox group, they recommended that their sponsors consider Dad as well, suggesting that he could eventually be a person to take over the church when the old priest passed away.

Processing through customs remains a blur in my memory, although it took considerable time, and I remember some painful shots that Nick and I were given. Dad told us as we finished there that he was welcomed to America by the authorities and given a $5 bill in US currency and a pair of nylon stockings for Mom as we were sent on our way.

As we left customs, we were picked up by a tall middle-aged gentleman named Mr. Korf, who spoke Russian to Dad and Mom. "I'll be taking you to Millville," he said as he greeted us, "to my in-laws called the McCloskeys. They will provide you housing and food. I will provide you a job." I understood his Russian, although his accent sounded somewhat strange, since Mom and Dad spoke Russian in our presence, and we were familiar with their accent.

Nick and I had gone to a Latvian school while living in Flensburg for three years, a holdover school from the refugee camp where we stayed once we got to Flensburg. Our main language was Latvian—quite different from Russian—and we picked up German while playing with the neighborhood kids. Neither of us could have held any kind of a conversation in Russian, however, since we spoke Latvian to our folks, despite Dad trying to get us to speak Russian once he learned that we would be sponsored by a Russian family in America.

Latvian proved to be a blessing when Germany was divided, and Russian families were sent back to Russia, only to be jailed or killed by the Soviets. A Latvian lady tried to tell the authorities who were sending people back that our family was Russian and should also be returned, but the kind gentlemen listening to our chatter in Latvian, only smiled at her and said that our family had Latvian passports, and as far as he was concerned, we did not need to be sent back. "Would you like to be sent back to Latvia?" he asked her. She shook her head and quickly walked away.

Somehow language never became an issue for us. We quickly picked up English in school, forgot our German and Latvian, and retained a general knowledge of Russian as we heard our folks speak it at home and studied it in our church books. Dad insisted that we speak English to them, probably realizing that children pick up languages faster than adults and told us he and Mom needed to learn the language also as soon as possible. Although he had studied English, Dad spoke it hesitantly and was determined to become fluent in it.

As we walked to Mr. Korf's automobile, I gazed at the sky and was awed by the tall buildings of New York City that towered over us. "Are all the buildings in America this tall?" I asked Dad in Latvian, and he interpreted for Mr. Korf, who frowned at my language but replied that New York City had some of the tallest buildings in America. He was taking us to an agricultural town in New Jersey, he told us, which had very few such buildings.

We arrived in Millville, New Jersey, after a four-hour trip from New York. Dad and Mom loved the large, fertile farms they saw once we crossed to South Jersey and asked their host if everyone farmed in the Garden State. "Pretty much so," Mr. Korf responded. "At least for themselves. They also raise chickens, which provides a good profit for our Russian people.

The McCloskeys, your sponsors, will probably have your wife and children work their large farms of tomatoes, onions, and other vegetables, which will shortly be ready for picking. You will be helping me in my construction business," Mr. Korf told Dad.

After meeting the McCloskeys, who included Manya and George, our sponsors, his parents—the old priest and his wife—and their three children, George, Marcia, and Tanya, we were taken to the two-story house on Newcombtown Road where we would live on the second floor. The main floor was occupied, to our delight, by my little sister's godmother Ina and her family—father, mother, and brother. The family were my parents' old friends from Latvia, who had been sponsored several months earlier from Germany, where we had met them after the war. They and their old parents, who were also sponsored by the McCloskeys, were responsible for our coming to America. It was a happy reunion!

Chapter 8

A New Home in America

G etting used to life in America had its easy moments and some that were quite challenging. We spent the summer after we arrived much as migrant farmers do coming to America from Mexico. The McCloskeys had large farms and grew a number of vegetables that George McCloskey took to market. When they ripened in the fields, Mom, Nick, and I spent hot, dusty days cutting onions, picking tomatoes and beans, and cutting corn stalks. My three-year-old sister sat in the middle of rows of vegetables and played in the dust and dirt, chattering and singing in Latvian, which displeased the McCloskeys, so I started talking to her in the little English phrases that I had learned from the McCloskey children, while Mom and Dad spoke to her in Russian at home. Marcia was the closest in age to me, and we hit it off right away and became good friends for the rest of our lives. Nick enjoyed relating to George Jr. as well, but Tanya was several years older than my sister

Olga and had little to do with her, so I tried to entertain Olga whenever possible.

Dad was working for Mr. Korf in construction and came home quite exhausted. He had put in an application to a company in the nearby town that manufactured glass products and was a good employer . We continued to live in the two-story McCloskey house and began to pay rent to the owners as we started to earn money. One day as Dad returned from work, he looked excited and told us all that he had a response from the glass company in Vineland, and they wanted to interview him for a drafting position, which he believed he could handle. "It will pay considerably more money than what I'm getting at Korf's."

"How wonderful," Mom exclaimed, and told us her latest news. She, too, had an opportunity to work in the cotton mill in town, where she had Russian friends who worked there and knew the foreman. "They recommended me to him. They said they would give me a ride to and from work if I get hired." That was the best news we all heard since we got to the States, and I jumped up in excitement.

"But what about us? Where will we be while you're both working?" I asked.

"We'll ask your godmother Ina, who is a high school student, to watch after you all when she gets home from school," Mom responded. "The wife of our friend who recommended me for the job said that she would be willing to watch Olga while I'm working —for a reasonable fee each day. She takes care of other children. I'll leave Olga there, and Ina can pick her up when she comes home from school. The lady lives close to the school."

The fall of 1950 came before we were ready for it, and it was time to get us enrolled in grade school. Nick had been in the fourth grade in Flensburg, and I was in the third. Mrs. McCloskey prepared us for school and what to expect when we got there. My first name was Yevgeniya, which she considered too difficult for Americans to pronounce. "Let's see what we'll call you," she said while thinking aloud. "Short for Yevgeniya is Zhenya, which is close to Jenny. We'll call you Jenny," she decided. I wasn't sure if my new name would also mean a "new me," but it sounded American, and I wanted to fit in, so I said very little.

"Nikolay can be Nick." She pointed to him. "I'll go with your Mom and sign you all in." From that time on, I became Jenny and my brother, Nick. Five years later, when we all took oaths of citizenship, the judge asked me if I wanted to remain a "Jenny." I told him "Yes, but please let's change the spelling to Jennie, with an "ie" instead of "y." I had been teased too often about being a "spinning Jenny."

School was a challenge, no doubt about it. When all you know is "hello," "thank you," and "good bye," being social with your classmates is hard. The principal decided that since our language skills were nil, they would put us both into the third grade until we learned English, and he'd decide from there what to do with us. There were, of course, no bilingual classes in Latvian or Russian, so we were on our own, which proved to be a good incentive for quick learning. By the end of the day, we had already learned some important phrases from the patient teacher and some friendly students. It was a fine start, and we both came home in good spirits, excited about the books we were given for the different subjects.

Our easiest homework was in math, since we both had Dad's ability for mathematics; English proved harder. But, with Dad's help and Mom's watchful eye, we were able to complete the assigned readings. Spelling was another matter, and in order to learn words, we had to sound out each letter, whether silent or not. That made us both great spellers, and both Nick and I won several spelling bees years hence. I credit my mother for this achievement, since she would test us each night before going to bed, pronouncing the words in her strong Russian accent but learning with us as we spelled each word.

With the help of a patient and compassionate third grade teacher, we both began to thrive in school, delighted to learn English and the world of books that it opened for us. We made numerous trips to the library, the used comic book store, and thrift shops to buy, borrow, or exchange reading material. I still remember taking a flashlight to bed each night, so I could read after Mom turned out the lights in my room.

Nick was promoted to the fourth grade after a month in the third. They decided to keep me in the third since my age was appropriate for the grade, but I didn't mind. I had fallen in love with my teacher, whose tact and patience were unbelievable, particularly after I was taking my turn to talk about what we ate at home and mentioned "black bread" as my favorite item. This phrase caused students to burst out laughing, since they knew only the white, cottony, Bond Bread eaten by that generation. The teacher patiently explained that I was talking about pumpernickel bread, which was made with molasses and was thus a dark color. She continued to be excellent at using my so-called errors to make them into cultural learning experiences for the class, at the same time making me feel less of a fool for my ethnic outbursts.

With Mom and Dad both working, we did not stay long in the McCloskey's two-story house. Dad found a five-acre farm with a small two-story house and a chicken coop, equipped with a well, an outhouse, and a fireplace that would keep us warm in winters. He came home one day to announce to Mom that we were going to purchase a home. "The land, with forest around it," he said, "reminds me of our house in Latvia."

"Volodya, you're crazy," my mom exclaimed. "Where will we get the money to buy such a place? We're barely making ends meet as it is," she frowned. This did not deter Dad.

"It's only $5,000," he replied, "and I think we can get that much saved in a year."

"Fine," Mom replied. "And how do you propose to come up with such a large sum of money right away to buy this dream house of yours?"

"I intend to borrow it from friends that we've made," Dad said confidently. Mom knew better than to argue with him. She shrugged her shoulders and walked away, assuming that this was close to impossible. Why would anyone bother to loan money to an immigrant who had been in the country for less than a year? She proved to be only half right, since the first people whom Dad approached were our benefactors, the McCloskeys. Although they had more than enough money to spare, the old Mrs. McCloskey was indignant that Dad had the audacity to even suggest such a step. "Volodya!" she exclaimed. "You can't be serious! What's wrong with the apartment that we lease to you? It took us years to work up enough money to buy the farm we live on today. What guarantee do we have that you will return the $1,000 that you want to borrow from our family?"

"You have my word on it, Mrs. McCloskey," Dad reassured her. "I will repay the debt in one year's time, giving you $100 in cash each month. Your apartment is very adequate for us, but we are used to having our own home, as we did in Latvia, and this farm reminds me very much of the land our house stood on in Latvia. I believe the Lord has saved it for us to lighten the sadness of losing our home and our family, not to speak of all our belongings in the war." This did not convince old Mrs. McCloskey, and she was adamant that Dad would not get the money from George and Manya, either. "Over my dead body," she said and stalked out. The young McCloskeys apologized to Dad but would not go over their mother's head.

Dad came home discouraged but convinced that other friends he had made in Millville would help him. As he described the conversation with the McCloskey's, my heart sank. I was not used to having Dad fail in anything he tried to do and having looked at the house and land he wanted to buy, I was already making plans in how I wanted my room to look.

The second couple Dad approached were the Simons, who owned a construction business. Katy and John Simon had become very close friends of ours, and their children were our good buddies. We enjoyed many Sunday afternoons at their house, and they in turn visited us often. Dad and Mom entertained them and other friends regularly. Mom was an excellent cook and could bake the most delicious *piroshky* (meat-filled pastries) and other delicacies, which our friends enjoyed. Dad was a great storyteller and had many anecdotes that he would tell after meals, and his beautiful voice brought tears to the eyes of his listeners as he sang the old Russian folk songs. The Simons did not hesitate to loan Dad the $1,000 he needed. They had the money, and they trusted Dad implicitly to keep his word. The same was true with the Burkovs and two other Russian couples. The last one to loan Dad money was Mr. Korf himself, who also thought the world of Dad and knew what a terrific worker he was from experience. He was sad to lose him but fully understood Dad's need to feed and house his family.

Within a week, Dad had his $5,000, as he had promised us, and concluded the sale of the house several weeks later. He also managed in a year to repay his total debt to his loyal friends, thanks to the farming and chickens he and Mom raised in their spare time.

Chapter 9

Fire Threatens Our Home

I came tripping down the stairs, taking in all the delicious smells coming from the kitchen where Mom was hard at work. Pigtails flying on the run, I was a ten-year old with freckles and a thin body in jeans, jumping several stairs at a time after a good night's sleep. We were in our new home for the first Easter Sunday, a holiday special to Old Orthodox believers and celebrated with more joy than Christmas. It was the day before our Easter, and Mom was baking a number of delicacies that we would all enjoy on Easter morning. This was the day before our long Easter service, and we had all been keeping Lent for the past seven weeks in preparation for it. The smells in the kitchen were so tantalizing that I could not sleep and got up early to see if I could help Mom.

Keeping Lent for the past seven weeks meant that we could not eat any meat or milk products, so our diets were quite limited. My brother and I took a peanut butter sandwich to school with us every day for lunch, which was supplemented with an apple and a bag of potato chips. It was plenty for me, and I was not complaining. Mom was a great cook, and we had healthy food for supper as well — lots of cooked vegetables, potatoes with mushrooms, and fruit for dessert. Oatmeal was our morning fare, without milk but with walnuts and canned fruit, such as peaches and peach juice. Oranges and orange juice were also on the Lenten diet, as well as toast.

The Easter dinner, part of which took place when we came home from an eight-hour service in church that finished around two in the morning, usually consisted of colored Easter eggs, sweet Easter bread, baked ham, homemade sausages, cinnamon-laced sauerkraut that had simmered for hours, and other delicacies, among them an Easter baba, a cheesecake made with numerous egg yolks and ricotta-like cottage cheese. It sat for days in a wooden pyramid-like form with Cyrillic letters (XB), which stand for "Christ has risen" embossed on the sides. We ate a nice dinner later on Sunday as well, but the breaking of Lent took place in the early morning breakfast, which was limited since we were so tired. Just thinking of the Easter celebration made my mouth water.

"Hi, Mom," I greeted her lovely smooth face with red cheeks from the heat of the oven. "I came to help you get stuff ready for Easter. I could color the Easter eggs. Where is Dad?"

"He's out in the back woods, honey," she replied with a worried look on her face. "It seems like there's been a forest fire quite a few miles behind our woods, where the railroad track runs. It's been a dry spring, and the neighbors are worried that the fire might move inward toward us. The wind is strong this morning and blowing east toward our house."

"But, Mom, that's a long way off. There's no way it could come close to us, could it?" I asked, worried that it might interrupt our Easter celebration. Dad had been preparing for it by transcribing the Easter songs like a scribe in larger letters, so the choir members could see them better. The ancient songbooks were worn and hard to see, and he was anxious to make sure that everyone in the choir could see the numerous Easter songs beloved by church parishioners and provide them a beautiful service. "Can I run over there and see what's happening?" I asked, hoping that she would not refuse me.

"Not right now, honey," she said predictably. "I need your help at home. Dad will be too busy to help me, and there's lots to do to be prepared for tonight's celebration."

I resigned myself to coloring eggs, after a quick bite to still my grumbling stomach. I heard fire engines in the background and became more anxious to see what was happening but knew my Mom would not budge from her position. Nick had awakened early and was already there helping the men ward off the fire. I felt that it was unfair to me to be kept back, but I could understand Mom's need for help. My sister Olga also needed attention, so I tried not to think about the fire destroying our first Easter celebration in our new home as I played with her and kept her occupied.

By noontime Dad came to get a short break and drink some cold water. He was sweating profusely and his face was grey with dirt. "We've been building a clearing a mile behind our house," he told Mom. "The wind is still strong, and the fire is moving quickly, but firemen are working on the other side of the fire, and the word is that they are making good progress."

"Is there any danger that it might actually come toward our house?" Mom asked anxiously.

"There's always the possibility," Dad replied. "But I've been praying while working, and I believe the Lord will let us celebrate his Resurrection Day in peace, so I don't want you to be worried about that. Just pray and continue to get ready for the holiday," he told Mom gently.

"Can I come to help?" I asked, hoping that Dad would understand my need to be there.

"No, Jennie," he said firmly. "I expect you to be Mom's helper since Nick and I are busy out there. You're more valuable to us here." He tried to praise me, but I derived no comfort from it.

Hours later, the acrid smell of smoke began to drift into the house, threatening to swallow up the sweet smell of baking bread. I closed our windows and peered out for the twentieth time to see if I could see the fire, but aside from some smoke in the distance, there was no sign of a conflagration. This quieted me, and I made a greater effort to concentrate on helping out.

By late afternoon, the danger of the fire sweeping into our home was gone. Firemen had been able to quell the flames and the large clearing the neighborhood volunteers had dug kept it from going toward us, protecting the homes in our area.

Dad came home tired but looking pleased, with Nick close behind him. He praised Mom and me when he saw the table set with Easter delicacies as he hurried to clean up. There was little time to waste, since the service for Easter started at five in the evening, so they showered and got dressed, joining us as we prepared to go pray for the rest of the night. Mom and I were dressed in our long black skirts, long-sleeved white blouses, with a scarf covering our heads, the traditional church garb for Old Orthodox women. Dad and Nick wore Russian shirts tied with a rope belt. Dad would bring Mom and Olga home after several hours, but Nick and I would stay with Dad until past midnight to sing the lengthy Easter mass. We persevered despite our tiredness—the Old Believers mostly stand in church, with occasional sitting on hard wooden benches. We looked forward to joining Mom in the early morning hours to sit at the table she had prepared for us. I thanked God quietly that He had spared us from a possible catastrophe as I sang the lovely Easter songs that night.

Chapter 10

Erie Beckons: Dad Is Ordained as Priest

We spent the next three years from 1949 to 1952 adjusting to life in America and enjoying our little home while trying to be farmers on our five acres of land. Dad also bought a small truck load of chicks to raise in the barn behind our house, convinced that they would be able to supplement his and Mom's income. They turned out to be more trouble than they were worth, since wild cats in the neighborhood got into the chicken coops despite Dad's efforts to keep them out and were able to diminish the final count of mature chickens significantly. Dad also bought a pig but swore he would never do it again in his life when he finally had to kill the poor thing for our use. I watched in amazement as Mom and Dad made sausages from scratch, especially as they stuffed the meat into sausage casings. The final product was delicious!

I loved the farm and the woods in the backyard, spending many hours roaming in the forest, lying in piles of leaves and listening to the rustle of the trees, burying boxes of acorns as if they were hidden treasure, and drawing maps for future treasure hunts. Being alone in the woods never put fear in my heart, except when sudden thunderstorms came up, and lightning threatened to hit me as I ran home, soaking wet.

I was growing slowly but reached five feet by the time I turned thirteen. My dark blonde hair grew to my waist, but Dad would not allow me to have it cut. The Old Orthodox believed that women should retain their hair long, and men should not shave their beards. I remember sitting in front of the heat vent for hours, trying to dry my long tresses. I wore it either in pigtails or in a bun on the back of my head, keeping it long until I became a sophomore in college, when I convinced a roommate to cut it to my shoulders when I went home with her for a weekend. I delighted in the freedom I felt with it short but had to face Dad's disappointment in me when I came home for the first time with a page-boy haircut. I was surprised that my college friends were disappointed as well, having become used to the crown on the back of my head. Neither they nor my dad were able to make me feel regret for having it cut, however. I enjoyed my new appearance and the fact that I finally "fit in" with the crowd.

Despite the difference in culture, I got along well with my peers at school and learned English quickly, soon forming close friendships with the girls my age.

One young girl, whom I admired for her sparkling personality (I was rather quiet and a serious student) told me one day that "she was not allowed to be my friend" given that I was a communist. This shocked me and hurt my feelings. "How on earth can you say that?" I asked her. "The communists killed my relatives, burned our home, and endangered the life of my parents. I wouldn't be here in America if it wasn't for their evil ways. My parents left because they wanted nothing to do with communism," I explained. I did not understand that the McCarthy era that we were living in made anyone with a Russian background from the Soviet Union suspect.

Although we were adapting quickly to American life, our religious beliefs and the fact that Dad was a strict disciplinarian kept us from socializing with our peers in most of the afterschool activities that took place. While other kids were enjoying sports and watching football and baseball games on weekends, my brother and I spent hours standing in church services on Saturday nights and on Sunday mornings. We were also kept busy after school, helping to care for the house, our little sister, and the extensive garden Dad and Mom planted in the fertile New Jersey soil. This left little time for socializing, and we both grew up somewhat shy and lonely for peer relationships but were outstanding students.

After three years of a stable and satisfying life in Millville, we were suddenly brought short by

Dad's announcement that we were moving to Erie, Pennsylvania, where he felt called by God to become a Russian Old Orthodox priest to serve a large community of Old Believers who had lost their parish priest. "I don't want to be a priest's daughter," I mused. "It's hard enough to have a strict dad who insists on observing all the rules and rituals of the Old Orthodox Church."

I cried myself to sleep that night and prayed that life in Erie would be at least as good as it was in Millville.

Chapter 11

Hiram College and the Russians

L ife in Erie, Pennsylvania turned out to be quite interesting, and I quickly forgot that I did not want to leave Millville. We retained our small farm in Millville because it belonged to us, while the three-bedroom brick home in Erie that we moved into belonged to the parish.

Dad was ordained by the Detroit priest, since the Old Believers lost their hierarchy during their persecution in the sixteenth century, and older priests ordained the younger ones. He immediately stepped into the role of a priest with a large parish of almost five hundred families, working tirelessly to tend the sheep and keep them from the wolves, who almost always seemed to be prowling around to disrupt the peace Dad had established when he took over.

Dad organized the children and teenagers, bringing them into the services by teaching them to read and sing in Old Church Slavonic, the language of the ancient church. I helped Dad to teach them the reading of psalms and liturgy of the service and to sing in the church choir, which was growing by leaps and bounds. Dad soon found it necessary to scribe the music in larger letters and musical notes, so all could see it when standing in the choir. He eventually scribed numerous notebooks filled with special songs for each service. He also wrote Sunday school weeklies to describe in English what each service and holiday was about. Because the entire service was in an ancient Russian language, very few people—most of them second generation Russians and Poles—understood the meaning of the service liturgy.

I turned out to be Dad's "right hand man," totally immersed in the world of the church. This left me little time for developing friendships, especially since excelling in school was also a family requirement. While my peers spent their Saturdays cheering for home football teams and watching basketball games, I was in church reading and singing church liturgy. My first date with a young man was at the Junior Prom, and we were chaperoned by my older brother Nick, who went with us and his date. To say that Dad sheltered me was an understatement. I simply did not date while in high school or prior to that, except for the two proms in my junior and senior years. This made me into a shy, lonely, and socially awkward person, and I could not wait to get away from home and enjoy some freedom.

"Jennie," my dad said to me when it looked like I would become the valedictorian of our four-hundred-plus graduating class, "we really need to look into the girls' colleges around here to see which one you might like best."

"Dad," I exploded at this statement, "There's no way I would even consider a girls' school. I'm uncomfortable in a dating situation and need to be around young people of both sexes. You might as well put me in a convent!"

I ran out of the room and cried for at least an hour in my bedroom. When I think back, I tended to overcome frustration and disappointment as a young person by escaping to my room and crying, sometimes for hours, maybe because the catharsis helped me to overcome unhappy situations and cleared my head when I was finished. It certainly dismayed my parents, who felt helpless in trying to deal with it and eventually resigned themselves to leaving me alone.

At the end of the crying session, I decided that I would rather find a job and forget college for at least one year. I would earn my own money and go to the college of my choice. I let Dad and Mom know my intent to not go to college unless I was allowed to attend a co-ed school. With determination and a little luck in the form of a hefty scholarship, I ended up in a lovely small co-ed college in Ohio, called Hiram. It was the perfect school to meet and enjoy my male peers, and I never lacked for a date. Of course, I could not bring any of my dates home to meet my family. Dad simply forbade it. According to the Old Believers, they were to marry only people of their own faith, and Dad strongly rejected any young man that I thought might make a good match for me. I finished Hiram and prepared to go to graduate school at the University of Maryland, where I received a teaching internship to teach English, while studying to become a college English professor.

The spring of my senior year, Hiram had a visit from a group of Russian educators from the former Soviet Union, arranged by my English professor. This was 1962, and our relations with the Soviet Union were extremely strained. The communists seldom let their people mix with the outer world, and the visit was highly anticipated by the small school.

"Jennie, don't you know some Russian?" my English professor asked me in class one day. "Mostly 'kitchen' Russian," I responded, curious to know what he had in mind.

"The visiting Russian professors agreed to have a session with Hiram's student body," he continued. "They will take questions from the floor, have them interpreted, and answer them in Russian, then translated into English. I'd like to see you ask them a question in Russian and see what their reaction may be," he chuckled.

"I'll do it," I volunteered bravely, wondering if my Russian was good enough. "But don't tell them about it ahead of time," I cautioned. "I have to be careful, since I still have relatives there, and the Cold War is far from over."

We agreed to have me ask the last question, with my professor calling on me when I raised my hand. I sat close to the stage of the auditorium, so I could listen to the Russians talking among themselves, and waited my turn to ask. When it became my turn, I asked the simple question of when they anticipated student exchanges with Russian and American students, given that their visit had broken ground for both countries' exchanges.

The Russians were at first taken aback but quickly recovered and took some time to answer my question, but they first all clapped to show their "respect for knowledge of the language," since they knew it was not taught at Hiram. When the session was over, they descended on me and demanded to know where in Russia I was from. I said I was born in the United States, and my grandmother had taught me what I know of the Russian language. I thought this was the safest thing to say, given my background, but my accent was authentic enough to question it.

The session with the Russians convinced my professor that I should proceed to study Russian literature. "English professors are a dime a dozen, Jennie," he told me. "And you have a talent most people would dream of." He asked his West Point colleague what the best graduate school in Russian literature was at that time and told me I should apply to Columbia University.

That was easier said than done, since I had no way of funding my education, and it was too late to apply for scholarship funds. It was even more difficult to explain to my father that I had changed my mind and was planning to attend Columbia University.

"And where do you expect to get the money to study there?" Dad asked reasonably. "You know my priest's salary won't stretch that far, and I've spent all I could to educate you and your brother. Olga is just beginning college, and I have to help her, too."

"Don't worry, Dad," I told him, not totally convinced that I could do it myself. "I have some money saved and will get a good summer job."

Dad just shook his head and offered to help with tuition if I fully funded the rest, at least for a semester. It took three jobs, including one as a night waitress, to gather the funds I needed for one semester. It was a long, arduous summer, with late nights of work as a waitress, days of managing a children's summer camp, and weekends of working in a local department store. Needless to say, I often wondered if I had made the wrong decision to go to Columbia. To be honest, what really convinced me that I needed to go to New York City and kept me going that summer was a movie I saw while still at Hiram: *Breakfast at Tiffany's*, with Audrey Hepburn. I found the party scene in Manhattan exciting and yearned for being at such a party in the heart of New York City.

My life at Hiram College was fruitful and enjoyable, but I yearned for a greater academic challenge and excitement that I felt could be found in a large metropolitan city, teeming with people of all cultures and backgrounds. I got my wish while in New York, experiencing several parties very similar to the one I saw in the Hepburn movie. "Oh goodness," I heard a tall dark-haired woman say to my date at one such party, "Utah, isn't that the capital of Idaho?"

And when my future husband and I were about to pick out our wedding rings in Greenwich Village two years later, I propelled him out of the store and confessed that I wanted a wedding ring from Tiffany's. He graciously granted my wish, despite having to take an extra trip to New York from Cornell, where he was teaching, to be there when the store was open.

My parents and my sixteen-year old sister Olga took me to New York City on September 3, 1962, with the trunk of my car filled with my belongings. My sister chattered most of the way, excited by the prospect of being in the heart of the city in Manhattan, while I sat quietly in the back seat of Dad's Dodge, wondering if I was up to the task of taking on a curriculum in Russian literature at Columbia, given a total lack of courses in my newly declared major.

Chapter 12

A New Relationship Turns Romantic

My head was spinning as I walked out of Professor Stilman's office. He was my new advisor—an elderly gentleman with a solid reputation who had published many books on the Russian language and its literature. He had suggested I take a full load of five literature courses from a list of many, which would give me a good introduction to the classics, as well as the more current Soviet writing. He also suggested I read my assignments entirely in Russian, so my basic "kitchen Russian" would be enhanced with more sophisticated vocabulary. Five heavy graduate courses in a new field seemed overwhelming as I pondered my options, fearful that my Russian was limited and in need of a good dictionary or two.

I walked slowly toward the elevator, deep in thought, and almost bumped into a tall, black-haired colleague who was holding the elevator open so I could get in. "Thanks," I mumbled gratefully, anxious to get out of the office and back to my graduate school dorm to think things over. "Did Stilman intimidate you with a long list of courses and professors?" the young man asked kindly.

"I think he confused me as well," I responded weakly.

"I've been around for a while and have taken courses from most of them," he said, but it didn't at all sound like he was condescending or pushy. "I'll be glad to give you a rundown on the faculty and what they expect, if you'd like," he surprised me by saying. "It might make your choices easier. Why don't we have a cup of coffee down the street, and I'll fill you in on the particulars."

As a beginning master's student, I was shocked that this good-looking, seasoned graduate student would even bother to talk to me. It never occurred to me, as he told me later, that he had watched me enter the office area and was immediately drawn to me. "Your blond hair and deep blue eyes," he smiled as he said it "drew me like a magnet." Normally a shy person, Jerry Liston was anything but shy as he waited for me to finish my session with Professor Stilman and made sure he got to the elevator ahead of me, waiting for me to approach.

"Are you sure you won't be wasting your time?" I asked, and for the first time took a good look at this kind, brown-eyed stranger who towered over me, a five-feet-two shorty. "Not at all," he responded. "I was just going to get a cup of coffee to stay awake, and this will keep me going until I can take a nap this afternoon. I've been studying for my PhD orals late into the night and am having a hard time staying awake."

We enjoyed each other's company over a good cup of coffee, and Jerry was helpful in explaining what each professor was like and what they expected, telling me funny stories about each of them. By the time we were finished, I felt like I already knew the ones I would choose and what they would expect from a beginner like me. We parted company after an hour of conversation, and I felt lucky to have met such a kind and gentle person, telling one of my graduate colleagues as I got home that I would probably never see him again. We both went out that night, enjoyed a great dinner, and indulged in several cocktails—two young women celebrating their first night on the town.

The next morning, as I sleepily opened my mailbox in the dorm, I found a message from Jerry, asking me to give him a call before nine. Since there was no "a.m." or "p.m.," I assumed he meant that morning, and called the number he gave me. After numerous rings, a sleepy voice answered, making me realize that I had awakened him. Embarrassed by my ineptitude, I weakly apologized for disturbing him and tried to hang up.

"No, no, no. Talk to me," the voice answered, yawning. "I need to get up anyway."

Little did I realize that the coffee hour was the beginning of a very romantic relationship, which later turned into love and a year later, marriage. Our first real date was a ride in Jerry's old DeSoto to see the sights of New York City from the New Jersey side, where we got stranded when Jerry failed to fill up his car with gas—the gas gauge was not working—and we had to hike along the Jersey highway to find a phone, so he could call his roommate to pick us up and bring gas to fill up the car. All this happened as darkness set in and numerous cars stopped to help, surprising me that the area was filled with kind and compassionate people.

Sitting on the wire fence along the highway while waiting for his friend to come, we got to know each other better, finding that we had a lot in common despite coming from two different worlds—he, an athlete and a potential Slavic linguistics scholar from Utah, and I, a Russian priest's daughter from Latvia, looking for adventure and excitement in New York City.

I also learned later that I was not Jerry's first love. He had been dating the daughter of a famous Soviet writer, who came from France to study literature at Columbia University. They had been a steady couple until I came along. I somehow ended up sitting next to Natalie, thanks to her maneuvering, in my Soviet literature class, and she struck up a conversation, anxious to find out more about the girl who had stolen her steady boyfriend.

"Guess what," I told Jerry that evening as we sat at the West End bar, drinking beer, "Isaac Babel's daughter sits next to me in my Soviet lit class." I beamed to see if he would be impressed that I had just met a really lovely French woman who befriended me and whose father turned out to be the well-known Soviet writer Babel, killed by Stalin after he was able to get his wife and daughter to France. Jerry almost dropped his beer in my lap and had to confess that he knew Natalie well and that they had been dating for over a year.

This did not stop Natalie and me from becoming the best of friends for years to come. I was even Natalie's maid of honor when many years later we met again in Austin, Texas, where she joined Jerry in the Slavic faculty for a year and left after her marriage to a wonderful professor she had met in New York City.

Chapter 13

Another War Brings Loneliness

J erry and I got married in 1963 in Teaneck, New
Jersey, on August 11 by a judge who provided a surprisingly good sermon on the sanctity of marriage that
was unexpected from his profession. I always wondered
about his reason for it and whether he noted something
about the two of us that was somehow different from
most of the couples he married. One may ask why a
judge would perform the wedding ceremony, when my
dad was a minister who had married dozens of couples during his twenty-year tenure as a Russian Old
Orthodox priest in Erie, Pennsylvania. Unfortunately,
Jerry was not an Old Orthodox believer and was, in
fact, a former Presbyterian who had become an agnostic
during his early years at Columbia University under its
liberal influence.

My dad had not allowed me to bring home any of
my beaus during my college years, since he assumed
that I would marry a Russian Old Believer—a requirement of my faith. In fact, during the summer before my

graduate school began, I had started to date what most in the community considered the correct match for the Russian priest's daughter, the most eligible bachelor in Erie. Luke was a wonderful man and a good "catch" for any Old Orthodox female. He was tall, good-looking, rich by most standards, and had a great job as an engineer at General Electric. And, most importantly, he was looking for a wife to start a family.

I had met Luke through friends in the community of Russians who belonged to my dad's parish, and we hit it off from the start. My summer before Columbia University graduate school was filled, during the few hours and days I was free from working, with interesting dates with Luke, a true gentleman, highly respected by my mom and dad. Luke tried to talk me out of going to graduate school and made it clear that he was interested in marriage. I enjoyed going out with Luke and always had a good time on our dates, but there was something that held me back from a permanent commitment.

I insisted on bringing Jerry home for Christmas against my father's wishes, and we drove from Columbia in his notoriously old DeSoto, in the middle of a freezing winter, with a car whose heater had stopped working. Cuddled inside my warm winter coat was a tiny black and white kitten, which Jerry had given me for my December birthday gift, when he learned that I loved cats. I had to hide this cat in my graduate dorm for a good twenty days before I could bring it to my cat-loving mom's house for Christmas. Luckily, I was able to take it to my friend's room on cleaning day; she lived several floors below me and had a different cleaning schedule.

Jerry, the kitten, and I arrived at my parents' house with trepidation. I had no idea how Dad would receive my current beau. Fortunately for me, my cousins in Teaneck, New Jersey, whom I visited often out of need for family warmth, had grown quite fond of Jerry, and Konrad, my cousin Ina's husband, had visited my parents and bragged about Jerry and what a wonderful person they thought he was. Konrad knew how difficult it would be for me to bring Jerry home and prepared my father for the inevitable when he last visited the family.

Jerry spoke beautiful Russian—a linguist with a gift for languages and their pronunciation—and charmed my mother immediately. It took a bit longer for my father to warm up to him and accept his presence in our house. We had been observing the Russian Christmas fast, which did not allow meat to be served for seven weeks, but my mom bought a half dozen pork chops, cooked them to perfection, and insisted that Jerry eat all six, which he did to please her. The visit was successful, as far as I was concerned, and Jerry left Erie to fly to be with his parents in Utah. My brother Nick helped him to sell the old DeSoto, which had seen better days but brought enough money to buy a round trip ticket to Salt Lake City for Jerry. My brother drove us to the airport, and as we returned to the Erie house, he looked at me and said, "I think you're head over heels in love with that man, my dear sister. I wish you luck."

And so it was, when Jerry and I decided to get married before he began a teaching assignment as an assistant professor at Cornell University in Ithaca, New York, that my cousins in Teaneck helped to plan my wedding—a small event with family and friends, minus my father, who insisted that he could not attend and sanction a marriage that was not with an Old Believer husband. He had tried to talk Jerry into becoming an Old Orthodox believer when he became fond of him and thought he might make a good husband, but Jerry's reluctance at the time to become involved in a strict, old-fashioned ritualistic church went against his grain as a free-thinking intellectual who did not know what he believed.

I was crushed at my dad's refusal to even be at our reception, but my love for him and the respect I had for his firm belief in his faith and responsibility to serve his flock helped to ease the pain that I felt. Dad was my hero, and of all people, I wanted him to be at our wedding. I kept reminding myself of his wise saying that the most ornate of weddings he had performed had ended up in divorces and the elaborateness of the wedding was almost a prediction of the unhappiness that would follow to keep from having any unnecessary resentments or bitterness about my modest celebration and his absence. To his credit, Dad met us the day after our wedding in our family summer cottage in New Jersey — the first home we bought in America—and blessed us both, wishing us future happiness and longevity in marriage. I remembered that blessing and the love he exhibited many years into our marriage, especially as we celebrated our fiftieth wedding anniversary.

As surprising as my Dad's blessing after the fact was, the attitude of my in-laws, who had not met me before the wedding took place was gratifying. They flew to New Jersey from Salt Lake City and greeted me as if they had known me a long time. The approval and love I felt during their time with my Teaneck relatives and my mom, brother, and sister told me that I was truly blessed to have married Jerry and become a member of their family. I couldn't help but wonder about the marvelous ways that God unites people from the ends of the earth, people who have no idea that He is sovereign and all-knowing.

I wish I could say that we lived happily ever after, but God never promised that we would have no suffering in our lives. Jerry, who had been an ROTC in college, owed our government two years of service. The Army had allowed him time to get his education but called him to duty in the fall of 1965, before he could sign another year's contract with Cornell. He was sent to Viet Nam to serve on active duty, leaving me with a two-year-old son and pregnant with a daughter, whom he saw for the first time when she was eight months old.

The loneliness that I felt during his absence was eased somewhat by the company and help from my parents, with whom I stayed while Jerry was in Viet Nam, and from my sister Olga. We had pretty much ignored each other while at home—she with her friends and I with mine—but having her come home from college to visit became a wonderful blessing. I needed a shoulder to cry on and a friend to talk to, and Olga filled the void I felt with Jerry gone. Dad even gave us a membership to the Erie Tennis Club, where we spent many hours battling each other in sheer competition and then enjoying pizza and beer in our favorite bar. The year with Jerry in Viet Nam cemented us as sisters and friends, and to this day we share the closest of relationships.

Chapter 14

An Airline Strike Threatens Our Reunion

J erry was sent back from Viet Nam in August of 1966 on an army aircraft going to Hill Air Force Base in Utah, near his parents' Kaysville home. This gave me an opportunity to visit with his parents and introduce them to their two grandchildren—two-year-old Nicholas and eight-month-old Christine—and to meet my beloved husband sooner. I had gained weight after my pregnancy with Christine and my mother's good cooking and felt quite unattractive, dreading my husband's reaction to this. The year apart took its toll on my self-confidence, and I struggled to find clothes that would hide some of my extra weight, to no avail. I found a nice straw hat that seemed to match my outfit and for some reason made me feel more attractive and plopped it on my head as we left Erie.

To complicate matters, an extensive airline strike made it difficult to find good reservations to the West Coast, and I had to travel with two small children for an entire day to reach Salt Lake City from Buffalo, New York, where my dad and mom had to drop us off in order to find a flight to Chicago, from there to Denver, and from Denver to Salt Lake City—three stops along the way with short periods to get to the next terminal. We left Erie at five in the morning in order to arrive in Buffalo in time to catch the flight.

Although my dad got us to the airport in time, the flight in Buffalo was delayed by the ongoing strike, so we arrived in Chicago too late to catch our designated flight to Denver. It was mid-morning, and the next flight that I was able to get us on did not leave until five that afternoon, so we had a long wait in a very busy airport. My store of diapers and food was soon exhausted, and I found it difficult to get around with the two children, carrying one in my arms with my carry-on bags and dragging the other by the hand. I was finally able to find a cart to lighten my load, and we waited at the gate of our next flight in case seats became available before our five-o-clock flight. We had no luck, and after what seemed like an eternity, boarded the plane for Denver. I realized that we would miss our flight to Salt Lake and prayed that I could find something available once we got to Denver.

Denver turned out to be a nightmare. The United attendant told me to try a flight on the other end of the huge terminal, and I rushed there with both children, carrying the baby and urging Nick to walk faster. Nick finally became too tired to hurry and rebelled by sitting down on the dirty terminal floor and refusing to go further. A soldier walking by caught my eye, and I asked him if he could help us get to the United gate in order to catch the flight leaving for Salt Lake. He smilingly obliged and put Nick on his shoulders, helping us to hurry to the designated gate. As luck would have it, we were just a little too late. The doors of the airplane had closed, and no urging by the soldier to have them open for us made a difference. "There were no empty seats anyway," the airline official told us, and left us standing at the gate, while he disappeared.

I thanked the soldier and explained that we were meeting our Viet Nam veteran who was coming home from the war. He was sympathetic but had to hurry to catch his flight and left us to fend for ourselves. "I wish you the best of luck," he said, as he waved good-bye to Nick. There we stood, tired, bedraggled, and hungry. I was out of diapers and out of food. There were no restaurants nearby, and the only telephone booth by the gate housed a telephone that did not work. I had not been able to get in touch with my parents or Jerry's. It was approaching seven o'clock, and I was beginning to panic. I had no idea how to catch a flight to Salt Lake or whom to ask for help. Everyone seemed to be rushing somewhere and had no time to spare for us. Airline employees were simply nonexistent.

The stress of the day took its toll, and I sat down in a chair with Christine in my arms, weak and exhausted. Suddenly, I found myself sobbing loudly, with Nick patting me on my shoulder to comfort his mom. My straw hat fell on the floor, and I ignored it and kept sobbing. The pats on my shoulder suddenly got firmer, and I looked up to see two airline employees standing by us and looking very concerned. "Ma'am, are you alright?" the man asked, while the woman took Christine gently out of my arms and cooed at her. "How can we help you?" the kind official, who was from Frontier Airlines and not United, asked. I explained my plight between sobs, and they led me to the Frontier lounge, quickly produced some food for Nick and me, and somehow found diapers for Christine, as well as some warm milk for her bottle. They brought a telephone for me to call my folks and Jerry's, who had all been worried since they had not heard from me, and especially when we did not arrive on our designated flight to Salt Lake.

To this day, I smile when I see a Frontier airlines crew in an airport and remember those difficult moments and the kindness they exhibited. Frontier took us on its next flight to Salt Lake City. The airline captain carried Nick to the cabin to show him the controls, and they sat us in the front row of the plane. We arrived in Salt Lake at ten o'clock mountain time, which was already midnight in the East, relieved to see Jerry's parents, waiting for us with outstretched arms. Jerry was to arrive the next day, and I thanked God that we would be in time to greet him as he came home.

That night I lay awake until the sun rose, feeling happy and anxious at the same time, wondering what it would be like to have my husband back and to stabilize our family. Jerry had written me letters regularly, which arrived late but were welcomed with tears. I had heard that many husbands had come back with Vietnamese wives but was sure Jerry would have been faithful.

When he stepped out of the military aircraft, I caught my breath, having forgotten how handsome he was, standing there with his captain's uniform and smiling at all of us. He scooped Nick up in his arms as the child ran up to him first and handed Nick an army truck. "This is like a truck I drove," he told him in Russian, having heard that Nick's first language was Russian, which he learned from my parents.

"No," Nick said emphatically in English, with a strong Russian accent. "It's a trok." And a "trok" it was.

Taking Christine in his arms, Jerry marveled at the curly-headed baby with fat, round cheeks looking questioningly up at him. "She has my curls and your nose," he noted. He then enveloped me in his strong arms, and we stood there quietly for a while — and I knew that everything would be fine. He had come home, when many like him never returned to their families, dying in the jungles of Viet Nam, where Jerry spent a full year.

Chapter 15

Post-Viet Nam Repercussions

J erry's return from Viet Nam brought much joy to the Liston family and happy celebrations of the Liston clan. My husband's family was one of the few non-Mormon families in the town of Kaysville, situated between Salt Lake and Ogden, and were highly respected by the community. Jerry had one brother, Paul, one year his junior, and a sister Nita, born ten years after Jerry.

Jerry's dad, Lee Liston, was a winning Davis High School football coach and vice principal. He had earned a reputation of being a man of high standards and many talents and was loved by everyone who knew him. He was lauded by sports writers as "one of those rarities in his profession who put playing the game ahead of winning." Lee's main objective was to build character among his football players, which included his two sons, Jerry and Paul.

I remember fondly his gentle manner with me, a young bride who met him for the first time at her wedding. While everyone was busy bustling with the final preparations for the wedding dinner, and Jerry was catching a nap after spending the previous night at Cornell preparing final grades for his students, Lee drew me aside and sat me by him on the porch in my cousin's house in Teaneck, encouraging me to tell him about myself. When I felt shy about discussing my hopes and desires, he prompted me gently with questions that were non-threatening but allowed him to size up the woman his son picked to share his life with. He never asked me why my own father was not in attendance at the wedding, and as we talked, I felt an immediate bond that cemented our future relationship. Without my realizing it, he was filling the void I experienced with the absence of my dad from the wedding celebration.

Our stay with the Listons was long enough for me to get to know them better and give them opportunities to relate to their grandchildren, since Jerry and I had been busy trying to survive as a young married couple juggling the demands of academic careers, a young child, and another one on the way. Cornell University, where we spent our first married year, was a long distance to travel to Utah to visit parents, and our honeymoon trip to Utah was filled with receptions and visits to meet the rest of the Liston clan, leaving limited time for family discussions.

Jerry's assignment to Viet Nam, however, brought his parents to Erie, Pennsylvania, prompted by an invitation from my dad to send Jerry off on his dangerous assignment. Mom and Dad Liston did not hesitate to fly to Erie, where they met my dad for the first time. My parents' effusive Slavic hospitality touched the Liston's, who were unfamiliar with such generosity and care, endearing them to their son's in-laws and the Russian cultural way of life. The two fathers, so different in backgrounds but similar in values, enjoyed each other's company as they learned about their lives and experiences, which were so diverse, and in their own way so colorful.

Lee Liston was born in California and educated in Nevada public schools, where he excelled in sports and won an athletic scholarship to play football for a well-known coach, Paul Rose, in Spearfish, South Dakota. Lee's mother died when he was ten, and Lee had to help provide for the large family, working as a "Call Boy" for the Union Pacific Railroad at night. Lee was the third child in a family of six, and when at age 19 he decided to accept the sports scholarship in South Dakota, his dad disowned him for failing to continue to provide for the family. Lacking money, Lee hitched a ride on a freight train in Caliente, Nevada to get him to the Black Hills Teacher's College in Spearfish, South Dakota.

Under Coach Rose's guidance, Lee became an outstanding half back and lettered in football, basketball, and track, winning all conference honors and setting records that stand to this day in the college. Rose considered him the greatest football player "ever turned out in Nevada." Lee met Jerry's mom in college, and they were married after he got his first coaching job in Lincoln, Nevada, with the help of a strong recommendation from Coach Rose.

After several coaching positions and training Air Force cadets in an extensive physical fitness program in preparation for WWII, Lee was hired as football coach in 1946 at Davis High School in Kaysville, where he ended up serving for thirty years and winning a football championship in 1949. He was also the school's Vice Principal, counseling many wayward students who later became solid citizens and came back to thank Lee for his guidance.

Jerry, and his brother Paul, played football for their dad at Davis. Both were chosen all conference, receiving scholarships to play for the University of Utah. Paul graduated as the valedictorian of his class; Jerry was co-captain of the team in his senior year and was chosen to play in the East-West Shrine game in San Francisco, where he deflected a kick by Paul Hornung (later a professional "great") to win the game for the West.

Lee's poverty as a child and the difficult years of the Great Depression led him to supplement his limited teacher's salary in a variety of ways. When money was lacking to buy Jerry a warm coat to replace his worn one, Lee won in a poker game to pay for it. Jerry told me that he never knew what his dad would acquire or "trade" when my husband came home from college for a visit. Labrador retrievers were traded for horses, and trucks for RVs. A ten-acre piece of land behind the house became "Peonyland" when Dad developed it into a field of peonies and sold blooms and roots for wholesale distribution. Dad's love of horses led him into a business of raising registered Appalloosa horses by cross-breeding Quarter horses and Thoroughbreds with "Appys" for show horses. Two of his stallions were consistent winners in the inter-mountain area, and one placed fourth at the national show.

Dad's horse business came to an abrupt end when his horse training partner disappeared with the Appalloosa champions, leaving him an empty barn and bills that took years to repay. When Mom saw one of her favorite horses at a horse show they attended years later and ran to Dad to have him call the sheriff to inquire about the owner, Dad Liston refused to do anything, telling her that it was an extravagance in which he should not have indulged. "Besides, I blame myself for possibly not treating my partner fairly," he explained. "Why else would he feel justified in taking the horses?"

Vera Cole Liston, a wise and educated woman who was herself a legend among the Listons, once wrote that not all of Dad's financial adventures paid off. When there was a failure, she said, his philosophy was to "get back up, dust yourself off, and try again." Mom was the practical partner who worked at IRS for fourteen years and helped to repay Dad's debts when they over-whelmed him. She also helped him in the ownership and management of the Kaysville Theater which he bought and kept for seventeen years, and, in his later years, in the development of several residential subdivisions from land he wisely purchased.

When we returned to the Liston house after greeting Jerry at Hill Air Force Base, Mom and Dad Liston advised Jerry and me to take several days away from Kaysville to become re-acquainted, after a year of being apart. They had arranged for a hotel in Lake Tahoe for us to stay, relax and enjoy the recreational area. I was at first reluctant to go, afraid that leaving our two babies with them would be too much of a challenge for both. I was especially concerned about two-year-old Nick, who only spoke and understood Russian, having spent almost his entire young life with my parents, primarily Russian speakers. My Dad had warned me that I should teach Nick English, afraid that it would be hard for his other grandparents when the time came for us to visit with them. I had rejected his warning, claiming that Nick would learn English quickly once Jerry returned and we would start speaking English in front of him. I was enjoying the Russian that Nick spoke so well, not even dreaming that we would reunite with Jerry in Utah. Jerry's Mom dismissed my concerns and reassured me that things would work themselves out.

They did. When Grandma Liston failed to understand what Nick was telling her so insistently in Russian
(Babushka, ya hachu kushat'- Grandma, I want to eat),
she fed him and it seemed to satisfy his need. When
Grandma insisted it was time to go to sleep, Nick would
joyfully tell her "Hokay!" but continued to play with
his toys until she shooed him to bed. Vera had a way
with young children and refused to be baffled by their
challenges, and when the stress of tending the baby
and watching Nick became too much, she would enlist
Lee to take him around their large farm and entertain
him with the horses and other animals. By the time we
arrived, she and Dad were Nick's best buddies, and
baby Christine was smiling at both of them whenever
they approached her.

To say that our week alone in Tahoe had its difficult
moments is an understatement. The time we had spent
apart, with totally separate experiences, led to some
awkward conversations. My life with the children and
my parents seemed so dull in comparison to Jerry's war
experiences that I was reluctant to talk about it, despite
Jerry's prodding. His nightmares scared me, especially
when I was awakened one night with his hands around
my throat, and it took some quiet talking before he was
awake and realized that he was no longer in the war
zone. One night he went crashing to the floor, taking the
window drapes next to his bedside with him. When I suggested that he speak to a counselor after returning to duty,

he shrugged off the suggestion, explaining that he just needed a little time to recover from being in Viet Nam.

Our love life was also on hold; I felt fat and unattractive when he described the beauty of the Vietnamese women and their lovely clothes. He had sent me a beautiful black kimono from Viet Nam and I had marveled that anyone other than a large doll could actually fit into it. He told me that his Vietnamese friends kept asking him when he would take a Vietnamese wife. It was a relief to learn that he had not succumbed to their suggestions as had many of his military friends. I learned that he worked closely with two young Vietnamese sisters to increase his knowledge of the language, but he insisted that they were both brought up as Catholics and had high moral standards. We managed to get through the week in Lake Tahoe, and both agreed that it would take some time to return to our former close relationship. It was a relief to get back to Kaysville and our young children to distract us from dealing with what appeared to be our deteriorating marriage relationship.

Our concern about our marriage turned out to be unwarranted. Once things settled down and we returned to the East to live in Ft. Meade, Maryland, where Jerry served out the remainder of his two years of active duty, our lives began to normalize. The original attraction we had for each other returned full force and we realized that our love had not diminished. We again began to enjoy the closeness that pulled us together as man and wife.

PART THREE

Family Challenges

Chapter 16

The Move to Austin

Jerry finished serving his two years on active duty in the Army in mid-December 1967 and applied for a job as assistant professor in the universities that had vacancies. Since it was in the middle of the year, these were limited. However, he had invitations to interview at New York State University in Buffalo, Syracuse University, and the University of Texas in Austin. He hit Buffalo in a huge snowstorm with temperatures below zero, so the interview that went well was put aside to explore the other two schools. Syracuse was similar, and by the time he finished that interview, he had already decided that the University of Texas was probably his best bet. The interview in Austin clinched it, and we decided that we were moving to Texas.

Austin was another world for all of us. I had difficulty discerning the Southern Texas accent of grocery store clerks and kept asking them to repeat their requests. Austin was still a small town and had few cultural events and international restaurants, aside from the TexMex ones, which we loved. The city was to experience its phenomenal growth after we arrived and were settled.

In order to enhance Jerry's limited salary as an assistant professor, UT had offered to accept my Columbia graduate courses, and the passage of the orals, to enroll me directly into their PhD Slavic literature program as long as I was willing to become a Russian instructor, with pay. Although I was hoping to use the UT library to write my thesis to earn the MA from Columbia, teaching three Russian language courses and taking three graduate literature courses—in addition to running our household with two small children and typing Jerry's dissertation drafts—left me little time to pursue my master's degree.

We enjoyed Austin and the uniqueness Texas had to offer, and our lives there were full and basically happy. We enhanced our family with two collies, a male and female, who added to our lives in their own charming insistence that we treat them as part of the family.

Jerry, who should have concentrated on finishing his dissertation and getting his PhD, spent most of his time running the Russian language program in the department, which at its pinnacle was one hundred students strong. I helped to teach in that program and tried to counsel him on its needs and inadequacies, doing my best to give him time to publish a number of well-reviewed scholarly articles. Our lives were more than hectic, and I was beginning to feel the pressure in my physical health. High blood pressure and ulcerative colitis were the result of my trying to be the "super wife" and to keep it all running smoothly.

To my relief, Jerry came home one evening to tell me that he had received a Fulbright grant to study Serbo-Croatian in Yugoslavia, something for which he had applied but did not expect to get. We packed up our house, rented it out, and flew to Germany to pick up our VW Combi that we used extensively to visit the Serbo-Croatian countryside and camp in its wonderful camping areas, and at the end of our year's tour, used it in European campsites as well. We drove it across the Austrian mountains to Yugoslavia, settling in Zagreb where Jerry had academic friends who promised to give him access to libraries as well as to fascinating Yugoslavs who were battling Tito's autocratic rule and lived to tell about it. The year in Yugoslavia gave Jerry the time he needed to complete his dissertation and allowed us all to catch our breath and slow down considerably. For me, it was a godsend. I had no specific assignments and enjoyed learning the language, meeting with friends, and raising our children.

Returning to the University of Texas and adapting to our old life was undeniably a culture shock. The Slavic department had experienced significant changes, with a new department chairman who did not appreciate the value of learning languages or linguists who taught them. Jerry had been warned while in Yugoslavia by friends that getting tenure, which he was up for, might prove to be difficult under the literature-oriented new-comer. To make matters worse, the new chairman also had a favorite candidate of the seven who were up for tenure, an old friend and former colleague, to whom he planned to give the one open tenure slot. His challenge was to find reasons not to give it to the most qualified professor in his department, my husband. Looking at the minutes of the tenure meeting after the fact, Jerry found that he was refused tenure largely based on the fact that he had fought in Viet Nam, something the lib-eral-minded professors who voted against him gave as their reason for denying him tenure. They were opposed to the war, and Jerry had gone in "voluntarily." He was also an eclectic teacher of Russian, one professor who loved the grammar-translation method complained.

Being refused tenure was a shock to my husband, who never even imagined that he might not become a tenured professor and continue life in the academic world. The practice of academic tenure's "up or out" policy was brutal. Professors had one year to find another academic slot but after that could not continue to teach in their current university. Several years before, this would not have been a problem for Jerry, since Russian professors were highly sought after, especially the good ones like my husband. He even had an offer to teach at Stanford University's excellent Russian department one year after he came to UT but decided he needed to stay at Texas and earn tenure there. However, in the last year of his profession, things had changed drastically. Women had won equal rights for tenure and salaries, forcing universities to hire women to meet their quotas, and a large influx of Russian Jews from the former Soviet Union competed with local professors, having the advantage of "native speakers" of the language. The universities themselves had also voted to dispense with the language requirement for their college students, cutting into the need for linguists.

The numerous letters Jerry sent out seeking a position had no results, except for several department chairmen who, like his tenure committee members, objected to his "fighting in Viet Nam," and emphatically stating that they would have nothing to do with such people.

I left my PhD studies and my teaching, refusing to be anywhere near the department, and went to work for the LBJ School of Public Affairs in order to help support us. Jerry found a job as an insurance salesman and opened his own office with Farmers Insurance. We remained in Austin, enjoying the city and all it had to offer, struggling to survive in our new jobs and to pay for the new house we had just moved into before learning about Jerry's loss of tenure.

Chapter 17

Saving Grace

Without realizing it, Jerry and I had become bitter after the UT tenure experience, and both of us found it hard to overcome the injustice of it all. But life goes on and keeping our heads above the water turned out to be a blessing in disguise. Making ends meet consumed most of our spare time and kept us from spending time feeling sorry for ourselves.

On one of Jerry's training trips for insurance, he ended up in a small Texas college in the heart of the Hill Country. About to go to sleep one night in his small dorm room, Jerry later described how he suddenly felt the need to ask forgiveness of his grandfather for failing to visit him before he passed away. This brought on the need to be forgiven by other people he felt he wronged and to forgive his academic peers for betraying him. Tears began to consume him as he lay in his bed and finally asked God to forgive him for his sin of disbelief. As he did so, he felt a gentle hand on his shoulder and saw a bright blinding light with the face of Jesus in the center of it. His tears stopped as he felt a heavy burden being lifted from his shoulders and a sudden peace, such as he never felt before envelop him. He quietly fell asleep, waking early in the morning as the sun was coming up, feeling unexpectedly different. He awoke with the strong desire to find a New Testament and to read the four Gospels. After a quick breakfast, Jerry found the college bookstore and bought a small New Testament. He grasped it lovingly and found a quiet spot on the hill of the college to read the Gospels. As he finished reading, he looked out over the quiet hill-side and again saw a bright light in the sky with a face that seemed very familiar.

Jerry came home from training a different person, one I did not recognize nor approve of. Gone was the strong, determined, tightly-wound husband I was used to, and in his place was a soft-spoken gentle soul with a quiet smile on his face, eyes that sparkled, and a confident walk that struck me as unusual. I spent an uncomfortable evening, trying to understand what had transpired to change him so dramatically and remember telling myself that it would pass away the next morning. It did not. From that day, our lives changed significantly, and I had to get used to a husband who behaved differently in every sense of the word. He was still the firm disciplinarian with our children, but in a much gentler way, and he infuriated me with his optimism and joy, despite the challenges which we still faced. He tried to explain to me how he felt, but I was too impatient to listen and rejected the religious books he brought home for me to read. Gone was the agnostic of years past. He found a group of born-again charismatic Christians in a small Catholic community and spent his spare time praying with them, urging me to join him. I steadfastly refused to have anything to do with it all.

I often wondered later why I was so furious with my husband for his sudden change in character and behavior, especially since I should have been pleased with the positive changes I saw in him. Life was definitely more pleasurable, and we began to relax about our financial situation, with Jerry insisting that "God would provide all of our needs."

The stressful job I had found as publications editor in the Lyndon B. Johnson School of Public Affairs after I left the university was suddenly phased out, especially when I agreed to join a group of female professionals who lodged a salary discrimination suit with the newly formed Equal Employment Opportunity Commission (EEOC). My salary as head of the LBJ School's Publications Program was half that of my male colleagues, who had less responsibility and the same level of education. President Johnson was credited with passing the Civil Rights Act, which established the EEOC, and I found it ironic that his school was guilty of what I considered shameful discrimination against female employees. I let him know this in a letter I sent him describing the situation from my point of view. He responded with a short note, saying that he would have the matter "looked into." Shortly thereafter, the dean of the School called me in when he learned of my participation and came close to threatening to fire me on the spot if I did not rescind my claim and take my name off the lawsuit. I remember my knees shaking, but I stood my ground and stubbornly refused—and was rewarded by having my position phased out, leaving me jobless. Since the lawsuit included the University of Texas as well, I quickly learned the risk of bucking the system of power. The EEOC ruled against my case, claiming that my male colleagues had degrees that were different from mine, and I was left jobless at a time when my salary, low as it was, helped to keep the family afloat. The arrogance of the powerful was clearly evident as the LBJ School hired a new editor to run the publications program and paid the man a salary twice that of mine less than a month after dismissing me.

Jerry was very supportive throughout and promised to help me find another job. I had taken a bad fall while at the LBJ school, slipping on water spilled on a highly polished floor, which resulted in disc problems with my back and neck. The back pain was bearable, but the disc in the neck had been affected to such an extent that I had to sleep sitting up to overcome the pain and eventually needed disc surgery to have the disc replaced. The stress from my job did not help to alleviate the pain, and the LBJ School took no responsibility for the accident, nor was it liable for it. Fortunately, we found an excellent surgeon who replaced the disc, and I was back on my feet weeks before anticipated and before Jerry's tenure at the University of Texas ended.

The last thing I needed now was the stress of Jerry's losing tenure and my being fired from my job. Back pains returned with a vengeance, and I found myself in bed not being able to move. Jerry kept bringing me books to read from his store of religious material that he accumulated after his born-again experience. Although I ignored most of them, one day while bored I picked up a book by a religious writer called Jamie Buckingham. His description of God's love brought me to my knees, and heaving with sobs, I asked Jesus to forgive me and come into my life to relieve the pain and hopelessness I felt. Like Jerry earlier, I felt a heavy burden being lifted and joy returning to my life. I knew then that our challenges in life were meant to bring us close to the Lord God, whom we had deserted in trying to make a success of our marriage and college careers.

Chapter 18

Enjoying Life in Austin

O ur lives in Austin, Texas, after Jerry lost tenure at the University were happy and eventful. We continued to live in Austin for eleven years, four years beyond our university employment. I was fortunate to fall into a job with the state of Texas as evaluator of Early Childhood Development Programs, working under the head of the Early Childhood Development Division, Jeannette Watson, and her deputy Richard Orton. Orton had come from the federal government in DC, where he was responsible for developing Head Start, for which he received much criticism after a botched and unfair evaluation of the program, which to this day serves low-income children in the country and is considered one of the best-planned programs in the federal government. Richard had met Jeannette in DC, and she expressed her delight in the program from the start, inviting Orton to come visit her in Austin. He ended up staying there and helping her to run the well-managed and busy department, delighted to leave behind the headaches of Washington.

Jeannette Watson was the recipient of a presentation I had given in 1972 for a proposal to evaluate thirteen early childhood demonstration projects in the state of Texas, funded by a joint grant from the federal government and the state. I was working at the time for a small consulting firm and trying to enhance their coffers with a hefty proposal to run the federally-sponsored program. My company did not win the contract since Orton decided to run the program himself with the aid of a Wharton professor he hired to evaluate its effectiveness. However, Jeannette Watson was impressed with my presentation and offered me a job to join her department as an analyst, with a generous salary. She was aware of my battle for equal pay for women and had profited from the statewide effort to insure all female employees received it due to the EEOC investigation my lawsuit prompted.

Richard Orton became my immediate supervisor, charging me to work with the Wharton professor and gathering data used to publish joint academic articles on the methodology and success of the challenging and successful project.

Orton was also responsible for helping Jerry find a job with the state of Texas, realizing that his linguistic knowledge could aid the Texas Department of Human Resources in developing terminology and manuals for their many customers. Jerry was happy to give up his insurance career and get back to what he loved best—linguistics.

I spent more time than I liked traveling around the state and monitoring the thirteen early childhood programs various Texas cities developed with the funds our department provided, but my absence brought Jerry in closer touch with his children, who demanded his help and attention while their mother was away. All in all, our lives were rich and harmonious, and we felt closer to our Maker than ever before. The lovely ranch house we bought at a lean time in our lives turned out to be an absolute delight, with a large pool in the back yard that drew many friends on week-ends and long evenings of interesting discussions.

Our main disadvantage in living in Austin was the distance from our parents—mine living in New Jersey (Dad had retired after twenty years as pastor in Erie), and Jerry's in Utah. We tried to make up for it by visiting during the summers and sending our children to stay with their New Jersey grandparents, where they enjoyed their cousins and an Atlantic shore house my sister and her husband owned. Our parents paid us rare visits as well, given the distance to travel.

On one such visit from my family, it hit home for me that life for them was not easy. My dad had retired without a pension from the church he served for twenty years and was trying to manage on his Social Security, since mom never worked enough to earn anything, and was finding it quite a challenge. The house he had owned in Millville before leaving for Erie was taken by the state of New Jersey when it also took more than four acres of Dad's land to build an exit for Highway 55, a major artery for the Jersey shore. More than twenty years after he had purchased the property for $5,000, the state left him a land-locked piece—less than an acre of wooded land—and offered $5,000 for the entire thing, including the house they took away.

Dad took the state of New Jersey to court at our urging and had his attorney describe the position he was in with the loss of his house and property, asking the state to add to the meager amount offered him. As he told us later, the judge was not impressed with the attorney's request for additional funds, and Dad could see that it looked hopeless. He would be stuck with attorney's fees and no additional money. As the hearing drew to a close and before the judge could rule, Dad asked him if he could say a few words. The judge agreed.

"Your honor," Dad said to the judge and those present, "when we left our country in Latvia, the communists burned our two-story brick house, killed our relatives, and we had to escape with just the clothes on our backs. When we came to America, I believed that we would never again have our home taken from us forcibly, but I guess I was wrong. America, the land of the free, is behaving no better than the country we left behind. The money the state is awarding me does not allow me even to build a modest home on this land-locked piece of woods they are leaving me, much less buy some property from our neighbors, so we can have egress to the street. It is truly worthless, and I have no funds to buy a home to live in when I retire in a few years." The courtroom was silent, and Dad, who had prepared his statement as a back-up, noted several in attendance with heads bowed, while others cleared their throats and stared at the bearded pastor, his starched white clergy collar contrasting sharply with the black suit he was wearing, sitting straight in the chair.

The judge awarded Dad an extra $3,000 to add to the $5,000 the state originally offered. While this helped, it was still not nearly enough to even put a down payment on a house. Dad's efforts to sell the remaining land proved unsuccessful; it was too close to the new highway with no egress to the road in front. When Dad was ready to purchase a home, my sister and I, with our husbands' blessings, pitched in to pay for the modest one-bedroom house Dad ended up buying in Millville near the Russian church, where he volunteered his services at retirement.

Dad's challenge now, as he explained it, was the ridiculously high taxes the state of New Jersey levied on his one-bedroom home, a sum that was equal to our four-bedroom spacious ranch home in Texas. I knew my dad well enough to realize that he would refuse any money I would give him directly. Once he and Mom left, I wrote a generous check to the Erie church where he had served for twenty years and asked the treasurer to provide monthly payments in equal amounts from an anonymous donor. I said I would send another check when the money ran out. As I had hoped, this made the church people realize that they had fallen down on their responsibility to provide a pension for Dad, and the congregation voted within a month to provide one, sending Dad payments monthly and continuing them once he passed away to my mom.

Chapter 19

Nick's Disappearance

O ur lives in Austin, Texas, took an abrupt change on December 1, 1977 with a phone call from my father in New Jersey, announcing that my brother Nick had disappeared and asking if I could come to Millville to help find him.

Nick, who was my senior by one-and-a half years, had always been close to my heart. As children, we were soul mates as soon as we could communicate with one another. People who saw us together—and we were seldom apart—thought we were twins. A cousin I met when visiting Latvia fifty years after I left, told me that he was our playmate when we were very young. He would come to visit us and had a hard time getting us to include him in our games. We would tolerate him for about a half hour and then give him his coat, so he could go home. A single child of wealthy parents, he said he was devastated.

Nick and I drifted apart when he signed up for the Air Force after an unsuccessful year in a branch of Penn

State in Erie, Pennsylvania, the city where he graduated from high school as a valedictorian in a class of 450 graduates. Nick was brilliant, and I tried to emulate him. In high school, he seldom needed to study for a test in order to "ace" it, while I had to put a lot of time into getting A's. He was under the false impression, I believe, that he could do the same in college.

Having been socially restricted by our Old Orthodox lifestyle, which precluded going out with friends on school nights and included praying in long church services on the weekends, Nick threw off these bonds when he entered college. He made friends quickly and enjoyed life hanging out with them. I was shocked when I saw him smoking as he drove past me with his buddies one day. Smoking was an anathema to my family, and I kept the bad news to myself.

Nick lived at home while going to college, yet we seldom saw him. He came home at all hours of the night, making my parents extremely worried and unhappy. After I heard my parents lamenting the fact that they never saw him and wondered what he was up to, I stayed up into the night, waiting until he returned from his late-night parties and chastised him for his insensitivity to our folks and their way of life. I did this on many occasions, but Nick never defended himself or changed his behavior.

When Nick's grades at the end of his freshman year were unacceptably low, he decided not to waste Dad's hard-earned money and signed up for the Air Force, telling my parents after it was too late to change his decision. Dad and Mom were dismayed, but I think secretly they were also relieved. Nick had become too heavy a cross for them to bear, especially when Dad, a pastor people admired, had a reputation to uphold.

When I consider Nick's adolescence, I come to the conclusion that he probably lacked the guidance and attention that Dad should have provided at some critical points in his young life. Dad carried a heavy burden in serving a large congregation and caring for its needs, which were numerous, and like some fathers, failed to take care of the needs of his only son. Add to that the sheer restrictions of his faith, Nick must have felt trapped and harbored resentments quietly. Nick was not one to express his thoughts or frustration like I did. He kept it all inside.

After his return from the Air Force, where Nick received training as a systems analyst, he landed a lucrative job at the Seagrams Company. He met his wife Jackie in New York City while working there, and within a year their daughter Jeannie was born. When Seagrams moved its headquarters to California, Jackie refused to relocate, and Nick gave up his management position, finding a less desirable job with a bank. Jackie never seemed to be satisfied with Nick, and soon decided to move back to Connecticut to be close to her brother and his family. She demanded a separation and took Jeannie with her. The separation was painful for Nick, who doted on his small daughter, but since Jackie did not want a divorce, he gratefully settled for taking care of them both long distance, coming to visit when Jackie needed some help in repairing the apartment they lived in to see his daughter.

Nick's unhappiness with his marriage also caused him problems at work, and he ended up abandoning his IT profession to join his brother-in-law, my sister Olga's husband, in Trenton to open a large restaurant Tony bought, with the help of his brother and cousin. Nick had no money to contribute to the purchase, and within a year was forced out by Tony's relatives.

Tony felt responsible for convincing Nick to join him and leave his profession and looked for a way to help Nick find a good alternative. While visiting our parents in Millville, where Dad had retired from his parish, Tony struck up a conversation with George McCloskey, owner of McCloskey's General Store and sponsor of our family to America. George was looking for someone to buy his once-profitable Mom-and-Pop grocery store so he could retire. Tony immediately thought Nick would be a good candidate to own a small business and offered to co-sign a loan of $20,000 as down payment if Nick was interested in a business with a mortgage to George and his wife Manya.

At first Nick refused, realizing that he knew little about running a grocery business, but eventually agreed to the deal George and Tony arranged for him. He moved to Millville, staying with our parents to save money. Dad even helped him with some bookkeeping, until Nick decided he no longer needed Dad's delving into his business. He also replaced Manya McCloskey, who was opposed to the idea of selling their business and had offered to stay on as Nick's manager and advisor. In her place, Nick hired a young woman to be his manager and probably hoped that they might form a romantic relationship. He loaned her money to buy an expensive sports car and entrusted her to handle the finances of the store, a huge mistake on his part, since he lacked a good knowledge of the store's small profit margin, as convenience stores like 7/11 and Wawa began to pop up in Millville, causing McCloskey's serious competition.

Thus, when Dad called me to tell me Nick had disappeared overnight and failed to open the store, he also explained that my sister Olga and Tony had come from Trenton to see what they could do to help. They found in examining the books that the store was in deep bankruptcy. The demands of their busy restaurant kept them from staying beyond a few days. Dad was counting on me to bring order to a chaotic situation and help to find my brother.

I booked a flight from Austin, Texas, and arrived in Philadelphia on my thirty-ninth birthday. Dad and Mom picked me up at the airport and brought me up to date on the situation with my missing brother on the way to Millville, New Jersey. He had been present at the Thanksgiving dinner with my sister and her family in Trenton, including Mom and Dad. The next morning he left for what they believed was Millville but never appeared there, and the store remained closed. They got in touch with the local police, but since Nick did not have a criminal record, the police claimed they could do little to find him.

I went to McCloskey's the day after I arrived in Millville and was surprised to see the store opened for business and Nick's manager there, acting like she owned the place.

"What are you doing here, and where is Nick?" I asked her after introducing myself. She said she had no idea but their verbal agreement was that she would take over the store if he should leave.

"Over my dead body!" I exclaimed. "It's a sole proprietorship, and as far as I can tell, you have no legal right to it unless you can produce some paperwork to that effect. If you want to continue working here and get it ready for business today, you can stay and be the cashier. In the meantime, we can talk about its financial bankruptcy—and what you know about it, since you've been managing it."

"The books are in the back office, and you can see for yourself," she replied, pointing to the office but did not volunteer anything else.

I examined the books and concluded that every part-time worker—and there were five of them—was owed back wages, and every merchant was due money. Desperate, I called George McCloskey, the former owner and our benefactor, to see if he could help me. The milk bill alone was $20,000 in arrears, and I was horrified.

George came over right away and concluded that someone was stealing money from the store, although he admitted that the profits were marginal and had to be monitored closely. "If I were you, I would get rid of the young lady at the cash register," George advised emphatically. "Her boyfriend is a former jailbird, and who knows how much money they both siphoned off while Nick was playing golf and she was managing," he added bitterly. "Nick owes me several months in mortgage money as well," he added. "I knew he would not last too long at this business, but I had too much respect for your father to bring him into this."

"George," I said looking straight at the weather-beaten wrinkled face, "I'll get rid of the cashier and most of the employees I don't know and cannot trust, but I know nothing about running a business such as this and will depend on you to give me some quick lessons. We need to keep the store running to pay off its debts, including yours, so I'll stay here for a while if you can help me learn the trade until we can find my brother."

"I'll be happy to do that," he agreed. "Wish your brother had been smart enough to take some advice from an old codger who learned the hard way."

As George left, I sighed as I looked around the large inventory of the store—from bread, milk, cigarettes, and toys, to magazines, greeting cards, and food, including a deli in the back—and prayed that Nick would return soon and relieve me of this awesome burden.

I remained in Millville until after Christmas, living with my parents and opening the store each morning at six and closing it at ten. By the time I reconciled the cash brought in, I got home by 11 p.m. George and his friends had a coffee clutch—his old fishing buddies— which met each morning at six to discuss the news of the day in a corner of the store, which officially opened at seven. Sunday was also a work day.

George was a tough instructor, but he taught me how to order the products for the store and took me to Philadelphia to buy fresh hams and deli meats at a wholesale establishment, where we also bought big blocks of cheese. We went to get batteries, toys, and cigarettes in various places. George knew all the distributors who came to the store by first name, and as they came into the store, wondering if they should extend any more credit to the business, he greeted them by introducing me as "the sister from Texas" who would make sure they were paid back their arrears quickly. I put the milk bill on a regular schedule of repayment to chip away at the large sum, learning that milk has the smallest profit margin—pennies on the dollar—but draws customers who buy other products.

I ended up firing all but two of the employees, after paying their back wages from personal funds, but I added some younger and older people I could trust because of their honesty and maturity. Firing the manager was the most difficult; her mother—a well-known figure in the small town—called to chastise me for cutting her hours to almost nothing. I knew that the manager had a large car payment and would find it difficult to keep up with the payments, considering the few hours I scheduled her, and after much grumbling and yelling, she left to find a more lucrative position, saving me the unpleasant task of firing her.

At George's advice, I enhanced the deli, adding home-cooked meatball subs to the cheesesteaks and other products offered. My mother and I took turns cooking them. These became very popular and drew more customers, including Joe, the owner of the pizza shop across the street. Joe bought the meatball subs, and I bought his pizzas—a good business exchange. We became friends, and when I experienced a part of the flat roof of the store collapsing after a heavy thunderstorm, Joe commandeered a crew of young men, mostly his friends, who worked all night to replaster the inside of the ceiling and repair the sagging roof, an event that repeated itself over the years we managed the store.

I slowly began to pay back some of the store's arrears and had my Dad handle the bookkeeping, sign the checks, and run various errands for me. He was seventy-three years old at the time but very quick and energetic and provided stable support. My mom, on the other hand, was a basket case. Nick had been her favorite child, and his disappearance put her into a frenzy of worry and demands to find him as soon as possible. I hired a detective who was capable but turned out to be too expensive, given the store's demands. Our best clue of Nick's whereabouts came from the gas and motel bills that arrived at our parents' house, telling us that he had traveled south to Florida and then proceeded west to Colorado and California. My attempts to call motel owners to find out the details were futile, given the strict rules of the Privacy Act.

Jerry was taking care of our children back in Austin; Nick was 13 and Chris almost 12 when I left. As Christmas approached, he took leave from his job, packed the kids in our car, and drove them to Millville to join me for the holidays—a long, two-day trip with many stops at McDonald's. They proved to be a big help during the busy time of Christmas holidays, running errands and watching the store for the usual shop-lifters, who took advantage of a bad configuration of counters and shelves, blocking the view of the entire store from the register and deli. They would come whispering to me that someone was attempting to walk out with magazines hidden inside heavy winter coats.

On one occasion, as I came back from inhaling a quick meal, Nick ran out to meet me to announce that a large lady was behind the cigar counter with a duffle bag, in which she was stuffing cigarette cartons. I bravely approached her, grabbed her wrist and shouted to the cashier to call the police. My cashier panicked and could not find the number written on a sheet posted next to the register, while the intruder grabbed me and began to literally toss me around. I ended up crashing against the front counter and knocking down a mountain of cigarette packs, as well as candy stacked near the cash register, while she took off with her duffle bag full of cigarette cartons. Nick, who was standing outside talking to friends, had the presence of mind to note her license plate number as she screeched out of sight, which we gave to the police. When they later approached her home, she swore that she did not own a car but that the license number was probably one of her relatives' who used her address.

George prepared me for the holidays by taking me to Philadelphia to purchase numerous batteries, stock up on cigarettes and toys, and fill the store to its maximum, using funds I took from our savings. McCloskey's would be one of the few stores open on Christmas Day, and he knew we would be busy. Busy turned out to be an understatement. A heavy snowfall covered the streets of the small town, and larger stores that might have been opened stayed closed. McCloskey's buzzed with customers, to the point where we opened a second register, which rang constantly. George's advice paid off in good profits for the day and helped to repay some of the store's arrears, including his mortgage payments.

Jerry and I began to plan our trip back to Austin. I had taken a month's leave of absence from my state job, whose employers were most understanding, but I knew I would lose it if I stayed away longer. Jerry, too, had to get back and school would be starting for the kids after the holidays. I tried to find a reliable manager but was unsuccessful. Manya McCloskey was no longer interested; her health had deteriorated, and she remained at home bedridden. Others I knew in the community already had jobs. I stocked the store fully and put Dad and Mr. McCloskey in charge of the part-time workers and impressed on Mom how important it was for her to keep busy making meatballs. I promised to check on them regularly and continue to look for my brother Nick. Thus, early on December 31, Jerry, the kids, and I headed back to Austin and to a more normal and regular routine, praying that the responsibility of the store would not overwhelm Dad and George, and that we would find Nick soon.

Chapter 20

A Hasty Return to Millville

During the entire trip back to Austin, Texas, I could not stop thinking and worrying about the store and how Dad and George would be able to handle the business that I left behind. Guilt can easily overcome a person as vulnerable as I was at that time, especially as I basked in the presence of my beloved family. Even the children's arguments in the back seat could not diminish the pleasure I felt of us all being back together again, and the long ride to Texas from New Jersey seemed short compared to other such trips that we had taken to see family in the past.

Jerry and I spoke quietly about the work waiting for us back home, while Nick and Chris compared notes on their exciting time while working at the store. The Austin house was my dream home, and I had missed it almost as much as my family, while living in the small house my parents owned. Admittedly, I did not spend a lot of time there, since the store demanded my presence from morning to night. I slept in the basement, where

Dad had built a nice bedroom for my brother, which I occupied in his absence. I went to sleep nightly, praying for his return and asking God to take care of him wherever he might be.

It grieved me terribly to later learn that he had spent some time picking fruit in Florida and had fallen from a tree, injuring his back and spending several weeks in a hospital to recover. It was simply incomprehensible to me that he had not gotten in touch with his family in the midst of his tragic recovery, and only the thought of his guilt feelings for leaving his family in a lurch could explain why he lost complete contact with us.

Several years after his disappearance, Nick decided he had to atone for his sins and to see if he could make things right again. He decided to travel to Austin in order to talk with Jerry and me about ways he could return to Millville and make up for his absence. Unfortunately, when he arrived in Austin and went to our house, he no longer found us there, but the new owners could not tell him where we had gone. Nick said it was hard for him to believe that we would have moved to Millville and left behind our busy lives in Austin. He knew how much the kids loved Texas and how happy we all were to be living there. The only thought that comforted him was the belief that Jerry might have found a teaching position somewhere else in the country. Failing to find us, he again headed south to find a job and a place to live.

We arrived in Austin and hurried to prepare the kids to return to school and for both of us to go back to work. The Austin house was a spread-out one story ranch house with four bedrooms and two offices, a large living area with beamed ceilings and a fireplace that covered an entire wall, and a country kitchen with a breakfast nook. The kitchen faced a long front yard that led to one of the oldest streets in Austin, a winding curved road—Shoal Creek Boulevard—that followed the curves of the creek bearing its name, which abutted our back yard. I cried unashamedly when walking through the arbor of bushes in the back that hid a beautifully landscaped pool with a huge palm tree at one end, near the diving board. The terraced red brick patio held two large in-ground grills, with doors opening both to the living room and our bedroom on the right. We had spent many long hours with friends who did not want to leave the warm summer nights with a smell of gardenias from bushes nearby and a pool that beckoned as the weather got hotter. It was not like any house we had owned or ever would in the future, and I loved every inch of it.

I called my parents to learn that things were going well with the store. Dad and George were keeping it going, together with the team of loyal part-time workers I had hired. This relaxed me enough to concentrate on trying to make up for the time I had been away and attack the stacks of work waiting for me at the Office of Early Childhood Development.

Two weeks after our return, when it seemed like things were settling down and the store almost out of my daily worry cycle, Dad called me unexpectedly. Concerned that something had happened with the store, I rushed to get the phone from Jerry.

"Hi, Dad!" I said out of breath. "Is there a problem with the store—something I can do to help?"

"No, honey," he replied. "The store seems to be almost running itself. I'm afraid I'm the problem this time. Remember how I had that appointment to have my cataracts removed? Well, the doctor who checked my eyes saw a spot on one of them and had me go to Wills Eye Hospital in Philadelphia because he was worried about the spot, and as luck would have it, it turns out to be melanoma cancer of the eye."

"Oh, my gosh, Dad." I held my breath. "What does that mean? How far has it progressed?" I asked in terror, my heart jumping to my feet.

"It's not good, honey. They took out the bad eye and are hoping that most of the cancer stayed in it and did not spread. I will need to get chemotherapy treatments regularly to destroy any cancer cells remaining. I'm afraid I'll be very little help to George with the store for a while."

"Don't worry about the store, Dad," I said to him. "I'll get Olga to help out, and I'll come to Millville as soon as I can clear things up here. You just do what you need to for your health, and I'll be there shortly."

I hung up the phone and sat down to cry, with Jerry patting my shoulder. I knew little about melanoma in the eye, but the fact that they had to remove the eye told me that there was a good chance the cancer had spread. I called my sister to find out what she knew and discovered to my dismay that the Wills Eye doctors had told her that Dad probably had a year to live, if that much. The cancer had spread and would eventually either travel to his liver or his brain. Melanoma of the eye was one of the deadliest cancers around, and no cure had been discovered to stall its progress throughout the body once it appeared.

"Honey," I said to Jerry, "I'm going to have to leave again and help Mom and Dad get through this. I'm afraid we have no choice here. I'll just have to take a more permanent leave of absence from my job and hope that it's still here when I return. Do you think you can take care of the kids for a while until we see where we go from here?"

"Of course," Jerry said quietly. "You might be able to close the store and bring Dad and Mom here to work with doctors in Austin. In the meantime, the kids and I had a good routine going while you were away, and we'll just slip into it again. "

As I went to the bedroom to pack, my legs felt weak. My dad was only seventy-four and as spry as they come at that age. He had seldom been sick in his life and always struck me as vigorous and invincible. And Mom, what would she do without Dad, who was like her father, husband, and friend all wrapped into one? She had lost her father at a young age, her son whom she adored, and soon, her husband. She would probably be worse off than all of us, and I hated to even think of the effect on her.

I had been especially close to Dad, as Nick was to Mom. Our common bond was the love of the church and its beautiful songs, which he taught me to sing from a young age. Each holiday service, I would come to Millville (and earlier to Erie) to help him sing the long services and to read the gospels. We always stood next to each other, and I could see the tears in his eyes as he praised the Lord with his beautiful voice. I simply could not believe that God was about to take him from us so soon, and I swore that I would be with him for the remainder of his earthly life.

As I began to pack, my thoughts turned to the time Dad was installing a floor in the attic of their Millville home after they became settled and fell from the second story of the house. He was shoving boards through the attic window while standing on a ladder and suddenly lost his balance. Seeing the picnic table below him as he swayed on the ladder, which had come loose on one end, he jumped to avoid the table and landed with his feet solidly on the ground next to the table, fracturing both ankles. He spent weeks lying in bed with both legs in a cast and suspended in the air. "That was sheer torture," he later told me. "Not being able to move was like hell on earth." He was seventy-two years old at the time.

I was also reminded of a happier time when Dad got a call from the well-known Russian author, Alexander Solzhenitsyn, who requested a visit to Millville to see the Old Believer church and to meet its priests and parishioners. Solzhenitsyn stayed with Mom and Dad for a week, discussing the Old Believers and their difficult fate in Russia, suggesting that Dad write a letter of reprimand to the Orthodox Church for its persecution of the break-away sect when its hierarchy refused to accept changes in church doctrine, scriptures, and method of crossing themselves. Dad, who was informally considered the titular head of the Old Believers in America, politely refused to do so, pointing out that relations between the Old and current Orthodox believers was slowly improving after centuries of enmity. He did not want to open up old wounds that would again alienate the Orthodox hierarchy and curtail the ability of the Old Believers to regain their churches in Russia, as they had begun to do.

Mom kept the famous author happy with her wonderful Russian cooking and keeping the press at bay, as the author had instructed her to do. She boldly told Solzhenitsyn that his Russian was strange, unaccustomed to the changes in the Russian language since she had left her home in Latvia. He laughed, and in turn let her know that her "classical" Russian was poetry to his ears—probably like listening to Tolstoy or Dostoyevsky.

I was dying to go to Millville and meet the famous author but could not leave my job. I had to be satisfied with Dad's calls and description of his activities. Dad told me that one day he and Mom had gone to buy groceries, leaving the author to himself. Coming home from the store, Dad stopped the car when he saw Solzhenitsyn pacing in the yard, dressed in a long fur coat, a large Russian hat on his head, and a notebook in his hands. He would stop long enough to write something and then return to his pacing. Dad asked later what he was working on, and the author replied that he was working on his book, *The First Circle*.

Sighing at the memories, I was relieved that my children were sleeping, and I could postpone the news of my departure until the morning.

Chapter 21

Trapped in Millville

I returned to Millville and McCloskey's just as the store was running short of products to be purchased in Philadelphia and in time to take my Dad for his first chemotherapy treatment at Wills Eye Hospital. Unpacking my car, I resigned myself to a long visit with my parents and was delighted to see Dad smile with pleasure when he saw Duke, our male collie, jumping out of the car to meet him. The two had become good pals when Dad visited us in Texas, and since we still had Duchess, the female collie back home, I felt justified in bringing Duke to give Dad companionship and provide me with a tie to my Austin family.

The doctors at Wills Eye had done a marvelous job in matching Dad's artificial eye to his other blue one, and an initially reluctant Dad, who was against removing his sick eye, was pleased that he had finally consented and felt quite normal with his one-eyed vision. "As long as that's all I lose," Dad said. "It's fine with me." He had not been told by the doctor about the honest prognosis of his limited life, convinced by my sister to postpone it until necessary.

Dad loved life and felt a very strong obligation to take care of Mom, fifteen years his junior, who had never learned to write a check or drive a car, although she spoke excellent English. He also knew that I needed his help with the store and was determined to continue in his critical role of writing checks and keeping accounts until Nick returned. I hugged him hard and tried not to cry when I first saw him; he was so dear to me that I could not picture life without him somewhere in the background, patting me on the shoulder and reassuring me that God would watch over all of us as we went through a difficult period in our lives.

Dad took the chemotherapy stoically, although it made him quite ill. However, he insisted on stopping at Denny's on the way home from the hospital in Philadelphia, so Mom could get her favorite meal there. The last thing he wanted at the time was to smell and look at food, but his strong willpower overcame the queasiness in his stomach, and we all enjoyed the fellowship and chit chat at the table. After resting from the trip that afternoon, he was up and ready to join me at the store.

McCloskey's kept me quite busy in the next two months, trying to find a balance between purchasing enough goods and not overreaching the income generated. I was reluctant to borrow any more money from our savings, realizing that the store had to sustain itself or it would need to be closed. I was current with the mortgage payments to George McCloskey, who stopped in regularly to give me advice on better ways to do things, and I could tell George was beginning to trust my instincts on what and how much to purchase. I was also slowly chipping away at the back bills for milk and other products. I added a middle-aged woman to my staff who had an excellent way with customers, hoping I could groom her for future management and entrust her with the store while I was in Philadelphia with Dad or buying new products.

The most difficult thing for me was being away from my children and my sweet, patient husband, who also took things as they came, understanding my need for helping my family. I knew his newly-acquired faith in God gave him the strength he needed to plow forward, and our almost-nightly discussions helped to give him guidance with the children. Chris had tried to be the "mother" while I was gone by keeping the house clean, helping to cook meals, and looking after the two men until Jerry noticed the stress it put on her. After all, she was only 12—going on forty, as he put it. She had always surprised us by her maturity at a young age. Nick was always telling her to "lighten up."

Jerry described her almost-hysterical lecture to him and to Nick about being tidier and cleaning the dishes after they were done eating, and when she finished,

Jerry took her by the shoulders and told her gently that she should not feel that she needed to replace her mom. All three of them would do that in their own capacities, he most of all. He saw her shoulders relax and gave her a big hug, reassuring her that all this was only temporary, and we would get back to our old routine of having Mom back soon.

I had left Austin in mid-January, and by the end of February, it became clear to me that I would not be able to extricate myself any time soon. Dad had regular visits to Wills Eye for chemotherapy, and as his illness progressed, he found it harder to handle the treatments. He needed several days to recover, and I missed seeing him at the store. Business had slowed down in the middle of winter and paying for utilities, which the old refrigeration equipment ate voraciously, was a challenge to keep up with. I found myself stressed and tired from a full day of working as I had to cut on the hours of the part-time workers to retain a profit, and by the time I came home—it was usually 11:30 after having opened the store at six in the morning—I crawled into bed exhausted. To manage with the bills, I had to keep the store open on Sundays, one of our best days in customer visits.

Adding to my stress factor were Mom's complaints about our lack of interest in finding Nick, which she badgered me with unmercifully when I came home for a lunch or supper break. Bills from his travels had stopped coming to the house, and we had no idea where he might be or how soon he would return. Mom kept insisting that she saw him in one place or another in town, and no amount of persuasion could convince her that he had not been in an accident, which kept him away from home. Since I was gone most of the day, my sick Dad had to bear the brunt of her constant complaints and unhappiness. As March approached, I felt the burden of running the store alone and found myself wishing for some help and comfort from Jerry and the kids. I felt trapped by the store and the desire to take care of my family, as well as make up for Nick's neglect and obligation to continue mortgage payments to the man who sponsored our family to America. I had also discovered in talking to an attorney about our situation that I had become liable for all the bills in the store once I started to sign checks as Dad became weaker.

Chapter 22

Uprooting the Family

In April, as I continued to struggle with the store and Dad's illness, Jerry was making the critical decision to leave Austin and join me with the children in Millville. He sensed my tiredness as we talked late into the night and understood my need to stay with my family as Dad was getting weaker and the melanoma cells began to intrude into different parts of his body. Wills Eye Hospital was one of the best in the country for his illness, and I could not picture taking him to Texas at this point in his life. I knew also that my mom would not tolerate the idea of moving. The store, too, could not be abandoned at the point where it was beginning to make a small profit that was paying off old debts.

In the meantime, Jerry decided to rent out our house and to join me with the kids as soon as he could. He had a contract with the state of Texas that he felt he could finish from New Jersey, which made the move feasible. The kids, on the other hand, protested vehemently. Both liked their schools, their friends, the sports they were involved in, and Texas in general and could not picture moving—even for a short time—to the "back woods" of Millville.

As Jerry began to clean out the house of extra debris and to schedule garage sales, I had to chuckle as I pictured my husband, who saved everything and could not part with any of his hundreds of books, forcing himself to weed things out. I later learned that our wonderful neighbors and friends helped him to make decisions on what to keep and what to sell or trash. Jerry's good friend and engineer Phil from across the creek told me that he walked into my husband's office to catch him going meticulously through the drawers in his desk, studying every small sheet of paper and deciding on whether to throw out a paper clip or two lying among the junk in his desk. He had been doing that for hours.

"I can help to speed you up with that," Phil said cheerfully, picking up a black plastic garbage bag, lifting out the front drawer of the desk, and pouring its numerous small contents into the bag. He proceeded to do that with the rest of the drawers, while a professor friend and his wife came to pack up the numerous volumes of books and store them in the attic. With the help of friends and neighbors, and with finding renters for the house, Jerry was finally able to extricate the family from Austin. He rented a large U-Haul to pack up what was left in the house and hitched a small trailer that dragged behind and held a car and our collie Duchess.

April 14, 1978 Jerry set out for Millville with two very unhappy children, who could not come to terms with having been uprooted from a home and a life they enjoyed. Millville, New Jersey, a small, primarily farming town with the majority of the population falling into the lower middle class, did not compare well with Austin, Texas, with its lively academic community, a spate of new and interesting restaurants and theaters, and the home of Willie Nelson and other upcoming music groups. Austin at that time was probably one of the most popular cities in America, and our family loved it. Nick ultimately returned to Austin to get an MBA at the University of Texas, which he financed after working for Marriott, following graduation from Carnegie-Mellon University.

With the family coming, I began to look for a house to rent. Mom and Dad's one-bedroom home could not accommodate the whole family, and we needed to be somewhere close to the store, if possible. A customer of McCloskey's solved the problem when he heard about our need for a house. He had an old two-story house near the store, waiting for a renter.

My family's arrival in April cheered me considerably, and even the challenges in the store could not dampen my spirit. We settled in the old house I rented, feeling the lack of our lovely home in Austin, but we made ourselves comfortable and the house marginally functional.

The store continued to provide us a challenge. A thorny problem I faced with the store involved our magazine sales, which were extensive. The store was flooded with every type of magazine from the distributor with whom my brother had a contract. Among them, and very popular with some of our customers, were the numerous magazines with pornographic content. When I first arrived at the store, I was amazed at the many boxes containing Playboy, Hustler, and other pornographic magazines that the boxes held, with most also displayed on the shelves. The first thing I did was to take them off the shelves and put them behind the counter, forcing customers to ask for them by name. In this way, I hoped to discourage their sales and to keep them out of the hands of the youngsters coming into the store. I also began to return unopened boxes to the truck bringing them in, but I found more boxes of the same offensive content coming into the store with the rest of the current magazines.

When Jerry arrived to help me, I asked him to call the distributor to cancel the pornographic issues. His call to the central office produced no results. They continued to come with the rest of the shipments. He then called one of the magazine competitors and asked if they would be willing to supply us with magazines if he cut out our present supplier. Once they learned the name of the company providing us magazines, they told him that it was no use for him to fight the mafia. He should just continue to provide the pornographic magazines to the customers, unless he wanted to see the store burned down. This did not sit well with my husband. He called our distributor and told him in no uncertain terms that we were definitely not accepting their pornographic magazines. We would just return them all.

A week later we received a visitor—a man in a black leather jacket who looked like a bouncer in a night club. He frowned as he entered and demanded to see the owner of the store. Jerry told me to stay at the register while he went to talk to the man. My husband, a former defensive back on the University of Utah football team, was not afraid of a fight. He strode to the back with determination in his steps, and I prayed that he would come out alive.

I got more nervous as a half hour passed and no one came out of the office. Finally, when I started earnestly worrying about Jerry's safety, he and the "mafia" representative came out of the office. Jerry shook his hand, the man gave me a farewell sign, and left. "What?" I asked Jerry impatiently. "What happened?"

Jerry said he thought they had reached a fair compromise. After threatening to shut down the store unless we continued to buy the distributors' magazines—all of them—the man confronted Jerry to see if he would back down. Jerry quietly explained to him that the store did a thriving business in all of the distributors' magazines and not just the pornographic ones. In fact, we lost money on the latter because many of our customers hid them in their coats and walked out without paying, embarrassed to have us note who bought them. Jerry also told him we were not the owners but that we were trying to keep the store in business for my brother and were ready to walk away from it at any time.

"What good would it do your boss to have us close down the store? He would get nothing out of it. Right now, he does quite well with our thriving sales."

"I can't go back to my boss and tell him that he can't sell any pornographic magazines here," the man replied. "He will have your store burned down, if not worse," he warned.

"Then let's try to compromise," Jerry told him. "We will accept two or three of your titles such as Playboy, and keep them where youngsters can't get to them, but we will not have boxes of offensive materials lying on the floor of the store. We'll probably do a better business with the few titles that are less offensive—and your boss will still get plenty of money and not even notice the difference."

The magazine representative could tell that Jerry was not going to budge and finally agreed to give it a try. "We'll see how the sales go with a limited number," he consented reluctantly. They would provide only the titles we requested—at least for now. Fortunately for us, that was the last time we heard from them as both sides kept their word. We stored the magazines under the cashier's desk and forced customers to ask for them by name.

Chapter 23

Criminals Cause Setbacks

When our Austin, Texas, renters left the house seven months later, we decided to put it on the market. Our finances were getting tight, since the store could not sustain us in any way, although we spent most of our time keeping it running. Jerry's Texas State contract expired, and he was lucky enough to get a part-time teaching position in Millville High School, when the Latin teacher suddenly retired in the middle of the year and no replacement could be found. Although Jerry had never taken or studied Latin, his expertise in so many other languages—at least six—provided enough background to teach second-year Latin, barely keeping ahead of the students. He also taught a German course, which proved much easier, given his knowledge of the language. Unfortunately, this lasted only until the end of the school year, when the school began to search for a certified instructor. Jerry had a Ph.D.but no high school certification.

The loss of his job forced me to find one with the local Wheaton glass company, as an administrative assistant to one of the company executives. My absence during the day forced Jerry to work in the store more often, and once when I came there for a lunch break, I found him standing at the register, reading a book in his right hand, oblivious to what transpired around him. I understood why the cost of shoplifting of our products had increased. The cashier had called in sick.

The sale of our Austin house enabled us to purchase a three-bedroom ranch style home in one of the newer developments in Millville, where the kids formed permanent friendships with the family across the street—two brothers and a sister. The older brother, Phil, later helped us in the deli section of the store, and Chris was in the same grade as the younger, Chuck. These neighborhood friendships assuaged to some degree the anger they both felt at "being stuck" in Millville, and especially when we sold the Austin home. For a year, Nick refused to join in any of the sports that he had excelled in while in Austin and moped around the house. Chris adapted somewhat faster but was no happier at being stuck in Millville. Eventually, however, they both began to accept their environment and resume their love of athletics. Nick became a serious pitcher and first basemen, while Chris excelled in tennis and softball. In his senior year, Nick played excellent football, which helped to get him to college. Chris was an excellent scholar.

They also helped me in the store, relieving some of the pressure I felt. Chris became a competent cashier, and Nick made excellent sub sandwiches as he managed the deli in the back of the store. I also introduced them to the administrative duties and management of the store, which proved valuable in their college applications in later years and in our being able to get away from the store for a short while.

On one occasion, Jerry decided that we needed to attend a Slavic conference held in Philadelphia in January. Both kids encouraged us to go and to stay for the two-day session, claiming they could handle the management of the store. We agreed reluctantly, having them promise not to take the store's earnings for deposit in a bank on their five-mile trip home. Nick had a moped and Chris was on her bike, following him, as they drove home in the dark. Contrary to our agreement, they both decided that the day's earnings could easily be put in the bank's drive-in window, which they managed to do well. Reprimanding them for this later when we found out and pointing out the danger they placed themselves in, Chris piped up, "But leaving the money in the office in a safe is just as dangerous." We realized that she was actually correct. We had been robbed once during the day when someone was able to clean out the safe in the back office on an especially busy holiday weekend as we were all in the front handling two registers. We surmised then that probably it had been the "jailbird" boyfriend of our former manager, who undoubtedly knew the safe's combination.

McClosey's General Store never failed to surprise and challenge us. While at the register one day, Chris was held at gunpoint by a man with a mask who told her to empty out the cash register. Remembering my past instructions, she gave him the contents of the register without a word and was content to see him run out with the money in his pockets, leaving her shaken but happy to be alive. The police came to evaluate the robbery, and it appeared in the local paper that evening. Several weeks later, one of our older cashiers was also held up in a similar manner and surrendered the contents of the register. Again, the robbery appeared in the paper. A third robbery a month later had us on edge, especially when our feisty thirty-year-old cashier tried to go after the robber, furious that he had the nerve to hold her up in daylight hours. Although no one was hurt, this was becoming a regular occurrence, and we were concerned for our staff, not to speak of the setbacks financially.

That night Jerry and I began to pray in earnest for God to solve our hold-up problems. Jerry had kept the papers from publishing how much money was taken after giving the information to the police the first time, which they provided to the paper. After that, it became an unknown figure. We were aware of robberies that took place in the nearby town of Bridgeton, which had problems with drug addicts. Some of them came to the store to try to steal our cigarettes and expensive magazines, and for the most part, we tried to ignore them. But stealing from the register and endangering the lives of our staff and family was a different matter. We agreed to keep the store and its workers in our prayers constantly and asked our pastor to do the same.

In answer to our prayers, the problems with the robberies took a positive turn. I was told by a woman, one of our regular customers to whom I had given a break when she was short on money, several weeks after the third robbery that she thought her husband was responsible for the first one. They were on welfare, but he suddenly seemed to have a lot of money despite the lack of a job, and she knew he frequented the store. I got her address and provided it to the police, who questioned him and got a confession. To my surprise, a few days later as I was purchasing gas at my regular gas station, the owner told me he had overheard a conversation referring to the store robbery and how easy it had turned out to be. This, from an alcoholic who bragged about his heist to a friend, was overheard by the gas station owner. Jerry traced down the name of the alcoholic, and he confessed when approached by the police.

The third confession came from an individual who was held by the police on a drug charge, and an investigation revealed that he was also involved in the store robbery. Although we never recovered our money, Jerry went to the Millville paper and had them publish the fact that all three of the McCloskey's robberies ended in incarceration for the criminals. That seemed to end our string of robberies, since we never experienced one after the article appeared in the paper. We had a few break-ins, but the store alarm brought police quickly and frightened the intruders, who took off. Jerry had to spend only one night guarding the store when the front door, which was glass, was shattered by a heavy object, leaving the store wide open to anyone passing by.

When I think back about our daily lives with the store, I marvel at the fact that Jerry and I remained married. The stress we both felt in running the business reflected in our daily discussions and arguments at home, which our children tolerated because they had little choice in the matter. We spent late hours closing the store and balancing out its daily earnings, which was primarily my responsibility. Jerry, the professor with a PhD, was stocking the milk, water, and sodas in our refrigerated cabinets and yielding a mop to clean the floors around it. As I remember hearing him tell our friends, "She walks to the back office, cash register in her hand, and yells incomprehensible orders to me about how she wants it all to be done—yada, yada, yada—and I ignore it all and go about my business." Instead of being grateful that this gentle, educated man was willing to share the nightmare that was McCloskey's and uproot his good life in Austin, I was chastising him for not doing a good enough job to please me. I shudder when I think about it and thank the Lord that we were able to get past it all. The local Millville paper even had an article, showing Jerry with a load of sodas on a dolly, ready to move them into the store's refrigeration units. The headline read: "Look who's Minding the Store," with a write-up of Jerry's and my educational backgrounds.

As time passed and no sign of my brother appeared, Jerry and I were beginning to get restless. We were ready to sell the store to the first buyer, but the fact that it was a sole proprietorship and legally not ours, despite the responsibility I bore for signing all the checks, kept our hands tied. We could not find a way to extricate ourselves easily.

Chapter 24

Finding a Way Out

Our hope to stay in Millville no longer than a year, when the rental contract on our Austin house expired, was totally unrealistic. First, the loss of our renters after seven months saw us unprepared to return to Austin. By then, I had lost my job at the state of Texas and Jerry's contract had expired. To go back there, we would have to look for new employment and a new home. Second, we were running short of money and selling the Austin house provided us a breather until we could both get jobs to meet our daily needs.

Most importantly, however, was my Dad's condition, which went from bad to worse. By February of 1979, the cancer had spread to his liver, and the doctors were giving him only days to live. The night before he died, I had a premonition that he would not outlast the night and was determined to go to Philadelphia to see him, despite an unprecedented snowstorm that hit South Jersey and Philadelphia. It turned out to be financially advantageous to McCloskey's, since we opened the store before the major storm hit and kept it open when everything else closed down. We worked feverishly to supply the demands of the area and flagged down bread and milk trucks to get our dwindling supplies replenished. We sold out of just about everything the store contained and were grateful for the unexpected money it earned the store.

I called Dad the morning before I left for the store to tell him I would be coming in the afternoon; he tried to discourage me, pointing out that streets were blocked and highways were partially closed. "Wait until the next day," he urged me. I was not deterred, however, and set out for Philadelphia at one in the afternoon, after making sure that the store was in good hands—my family's. As Dad had feared, I was stopped numerous times on streets that were totally covered with snow and impassable but found other routes to keep going. A one-and-a-half hour drive to Philadelphia took me seven hours, but I arrived at Wills Eye hospital around eight that evening, to find my mother and sister already there. They had come from Trenton and also had to battle the snow and closed streets. We spent the night talking to Dad and watching him fade out of our lives. My sister Olga reminded him that it was the 21st of February, her birthday, and we had to celebrate the occasion. He feebly tried to accommodate us. By two in the morning, Dad passed from our lives, and we all sat there shocked, despite the knowledge that he was going to his Maker.

Dad was seventy-four years old, and if not for the melanoma, in good health throughout his life, which was dedicated to God and to making life meaningful for those around him.

Dad's funeral brought two busloads of his former parishioners from Erie, all wanting to pay their last respects to him. His open coffin was placed in the small Millville church where he faithfully served the parish after retiring from Erie. Always the peacemaker, Dad deferred to the young man who had become the priest of the church and stayed in the background to provide his services as needed. He taught the young people who were interested in reading and singing, and scribed several songbooks for the choir to make it easier for them to see the music. He was there at every service, providing his lovely voice to enhance the singing and reading.

I walked into the quiet, cool church as he lay there to take my turn in chanting the liturgy as was the custom of the church and was taken by the soft smile on his face, as if he had already met his Maker. I wanted to cry but instead found myself full of joy and began to chant in a sing-song voice that was filled with emotion and an unbelievable peace. I can't remember feeling such joy ever before. I told my dad how much I loved him and how happy I was that his suffering was at an end. I promised to take care of Mom and help to find my brother. I was happy for my dad; he deserved to leave this crazy chaotic world and celebrate a new life that had no sorrow, no evil, and no disease.

Mom, who was in a daze as Dad was laid to rest, was inconsolable after the funeral and grieved to the point of almost joining him, forcing us to comfort her and keep her as calm as possible. Since she was quite helpless to tend to her own needs and stubborn enough to refuse to leave her home, we felt obligated to see her through her difficult mourning period, especially since my brother had not returned, and we were no closer to finding him than ever before. With Dad's passing, I had to take over signing checks for the bills and invoices of the store, which legally made me responsible for all its debts, and I was determined to pay them off.

We continued to struggle with the store for another four years—five altogether. I was working outside the store almost full time, and Jerry decided to go back to a local college to get his teaching certificate. He had learned a good lesson with his part-time experience in Millville High. The school still had a need for a French and German teacher, both languages Jerry knew well. He was determined to get the certificate in one summer, taking four courses he needed to attain it. With certificate in hand, he applied to the high school to teach French and German, and was hired for several years before they found a teacher who was fresh out of college and did not require the salary of a PhD.

Our children graduated from Millville High School a year apart, and with good grades and excellent athletic ability, earned scholarships to fine colleges. We had no money to send them to college, given the requirements of the store, but God saw to it that they both attended the best schools. Nick was courted by Carnegie-Mellon because of his excellence in football and joined the team when he entered college. Following graduation, he worked to finance himself through the University of Texas MBA program. Chris, who was outstanding in scholarship and the salutatorian of her class, also played excellent tennis, a plus for Bucknell, where she spent her next four years. After working on Wall Street at Drexel Burnham Lambert, where she complained that the elevator in the building was her worst enemy (it was too slow for her), she left the company to earn an MBA from Harvard.

We continued to work and run the store, which by then had come out of debt and was holding its own. Given our religious beliefs, we decided to close it on Sundays, which saw our profits dip and caused quite a bit of anger on the part of our loyal customers, but the store continued to do well the rest of the week.

"Jennie," my husband said to me five years into the store, "it's time for us to leave Millville and get on with our professional lives."

I thoroughly agreed and proceeded to plan a departure, which was not an easy task. Mom was still having difficulties and depending on us to keep her going. The store could not be closed easily, without abandoning George McCloskey and his dependence on the mortgage money. Worst of all, we could not legally sell the business. It was a sole proprietorship belonging to my brother, and we had no idea where to find him.

While the majority of the debts of the store had been paid, and the store was on a current schedule, my brother-in-law's co-signature of the $20,000 loan to my brother would leave him responsible for the debt if we closed down the business, and legally mine since I was signing all the checks. The rest of the mortgage to George was also in question and had to be settled with a final payment. Neither of us could afford the costs or the loss for which we would be responsible. The attorney I consulted felt sorry for me but could not come up with a solution. He referred me to a specialist in foreclosures, who miraculously found a New Jersey law that provided for a guardian to function in place of a missing owner if the owner had been gone for a certain period of time, which Nick had been. The law required that a judge rule on the case after examining the books of the business to make sure that no improprieties had taken place.

Jerry and I appeared before a judge, after hiring an accountant to examine the store's books and presenting the results to the judge. After we explained our situation to the judge, he asked us what we wanted to do with the store. "Sell it for my brother and pay off the rest of his debts," I replied. The judge directed us to hire a real estate firm to represent the business and put it on the market. In the meantime, he made us guardians of the store and insisted that we pay ourselves a salary, which we had not done in the past.

We walked out of court and breathed a sigh of relief, feeling a big weight lifted from our shoulders. The store was put on the market the following week, and we waited in anticipation for a buyer. Since we did not own the store, we could not provide the potential buyer a mortgage and the ability to pay it off. The US economy was floundering and interest rates for borrowing money were at an all-time high—up to 17 percent. The few potential buyers who checked into the purchase of the store were understandably discouraged by the business market and high interest rates. The store remained open without a single buyer being brought by the real estate company for an entire year. We were trapped and felt that we would be stuck with the store for the rest of our lives—or until we could find my brother.

One night after talking to the real estate company representative whose contract expired, Jerry and I decided it was time once again for extensive prayer. We sat together holding hands and praying that God would find us an experienced buyer who could afford the store, that the buyer would profit from the store, and that the high interest rates would not discourage him. The next day, I developed an advertisement for the *Atlantic City Press*, and we sent it in on a prayer. Nothing happened in the next few weeks; we did not have a response to our week-long ad. However, in the following week, we were approached by two potential buyers. One of them had to be rejected, since he could not afford the business. The second, a woman who had run a store in Atlantic City, appeared promising. She had watched customers coming in and out of the store and decided it had potential. Her husband was a car dealer and had money to invest in a business, which he wanted to buy for her. There was one major hitch: she wanted to take over the mortgage Nick had with George McCloskey with an interest rate of six percent. I felt dejected, knowing how George would react to that but told her that I would check with the former owner.

When I approached George with the news of the potential buyer who wanted to take over Nick's mortgage and pay George its interest rate, George let out a loud guffaw. "You must be kidding, Jennie," he said to me. "Why would I even consider it when I can get up to 17 percent for the mortgage?"

"No, you can't, George," I insisted. "No one can afford that these days, and the store cannot be sold unless you agree to it. Jerry and I are ready to close it down and get on with our lives, and that will give you nothing but an old, worn-out building—unless you want to take over the store yourself."

"Of course, I don't," he almost yelled it out. "I'm much too old for that. You sure drive a hard bargain," he said, after thinking about my proposition. "If I didn't think so much of your mom and dad, I would never agree to this crazy proposal. First, I want to meet this woman to make sure that she is qualified to run the business and honest enough to pay me the mortgage on a regular basis. Then we can talk further." I quickly arranged for the meeting and held my breath.

To our delight, George McCloskey liked the potential buyer and saw wisdom in continuing to get his mortgage payments. He was willing to have her take over Nick's mortgage if it guaranteed the sale of the store. With the help of our attorney, we prepared papers for the purchase, making sure that the profit margin included a payback for the $20,000 loan that was outstanding to my brother-in-law. In fact, the price of the store barely took care of the loan amount and some other smaller debts that needed to be paid. We were grateful, however, and went to the closing in anticipation of being free once again.

Freedom never comes easy, as we found out during the purchase negotiations. The agreement included a full stocking of the store, which took away from some of the profits, and fixing the flat roof, which had given us many headaches during storms. At one point in the negotiations, the buyer's attorney turned to the husband of the future store owner and warned him that he was making a big mistake to buy McCloskey's for his wife. There was silence all around, broken after a few minutes by the husband. "I promised my wife I would get her a store, and I don't intend to break that promise," he said with conviction.

"So be it," their attorney retorted. "But don't blame me if it goes bankrupt. It's an old store, surrounded by modern 7/11s, and its life is bound to be limited." We proceeded to sign the agreement, which still had to be approved by the judge who gave us the ability to sell it, but our hearts were grateful to God for releasing us from the burden that had become almost too much to bear.

In retrospect, I need to say that it turned out to be as we had prayed so specifically. The new owner did well with the store, which she kept for the next six years. She paid off George's mortgage and sold the store profitably. We went on with our lives and got back to our professional jobs, having gained from the store experience in developing greater strength of character, which served us well in our future years. The experience our children had in helping to run the store helped them in their acceptance to college and graduate schools as well.

Chapter 25

We Find My Brother

Nick's disappearance lasted almost seventeen years, during which my mother grieved for his loss, hoping that he would appear any day. Neither she nor I believed that he was dead but both hoped that wherever he was, life was being kind to him.

My mother continued to keep in touch with Nick's wife Jackie and daughter Jeannie, and as the young girl grew, she spent many weeks with her grandmother. She and my sister's daughter, Toni, became close friends, spending many summers together at Olga's and Tony's summer home on the beach. Jeannie loved her grandmother and hated to see the agony she went through with Nick's disapparance. Jeannie was determined as she grew up that she would find her dad for her grandmother.

When Jeannie was about to turn seventeen, she urged her mother to help her find Nick, possibly through Social Security. Jackie called Social Security to see if Nick's Social Security number was still being utilized and found out that someone was using it, but she could get no further information from the agency because of its strict privacy laws. This did not stop Jeannie from calling as well and begging the woman on the other end to forward a letter from her to her dad. She explained the situation to her interlocutor and fortunately for her, the woman agreed to do just that.

When Nick, who was living in Tampa, Florida, at the time, received the letter from his long-absent daughter, he was shocked but not psychologically prepared for a meeting. He realized that her birthday was coming and ordered a dozen roses to be sent to her on her seventeenth birthday. When the roses arrived, Jeannie desperately tried to elicit the address of the sender from the flower shop but had no success. She only knew that they came from Tampa, Florida.

Jeannie was discouraged but still determined, happy that she discovered he was alive and the state where he lived. She did not want to tell her grandmother so as not to raise her hopes too high, in case she was still unsuccessful in finding him. One day, as she was watching the Oprah Winfrey show, Jeannie found out from the show that if someone had a missing loved one and had his/her Social Security number and knew the state the missing person lived in, they could send a dollar to that state's Division of Motor Vehicles and request the address of that person.

"Mom," she said in excitement. "Do you have Dad's Social Security number? I think I know how to get his address." Jackie gave her the Social Security number and hoped Jeannie would not be disappointed again. True to Oprah's show information, the Florida DMV sent Jeannie her dad's address in response to her request. Overjoyed, Jeannie immediately wrote to Nick to tell him she was coming to meet him in Florida. Nick was not prepared to have her visit his trailer home and gave her an address of a restaurant where they could meet for lunch.

Seventeen years almost to the day he disappeared, father and daughter had their reunion, an awkward and tearful meeting of two people who were practically strangers. Jeannie later commented, "He looked so different from what I expected," having pictured her dad much taller and younger.

Nick later said, "She is a beauty! How could I have waited so long to see her?"

"You must come to Millville to see Grandmother, who has been suffering all these years not knowing if you were alive," Jeannie told her dad. His hesitation surprised and disappointed her. "Well, not right away," she conceded, "but soon. Grandpa passed away, and we don't know how long Grandma will be around," Jeannie scolded her father.

"I will; I will," he replied. "But give me some time to absorb all this."

Jeannie got her dad's phone number and left to go back to Connecticut, somewhat disappointed and unsure of what her dad would do. Once home, she described her meeting to Olga, and I immediately requested Nick's phone number.

I called Nick within a week and had a tearful reunion with him on the phone. I wanted to be sure that he knew we solved the problem of the store, so it would not impede his decision to come see Mom. Like Jeannie, I was concerned about her health and longevity.

"I found out inadvertently that you and Jerry were taking care of the store," he told me. "A visitor from Vineland came to the Campground I was managing, and I asked him about McCloskey's General Store. He told me that the guy who owned it disappeared, and his sister came from Texas to take it over. I felt horrible that you and Jerry were stuck with it and had left your careers, and decided I definitely could not face you," he related.

I sent Nick a round-trip ticket to the Dulles International Airport near my home in Virginia at the time, making sure that he came as promised. Mom and I met him there. Seventeen years and a hard life had taken its toll on Nick, and as he came to meet us, I was shocked by his grey hair, bent-over body, and the many lines in his face, but his smile was the same. Mom and I could not stop hugging him, unable to believe that he was finally with us.

Nick spent time with all of us, including my sister and her husband and family. He came back in the summer to visit with Mom and Jeannie, but he continued to live in Florida, where he had friends, a job, and a new life he was used to. He died at the young age of sixty-four of emphysema, brought on by his many years of smoking and the dampness of the Florida climate. We all mourned his loss and buried him next to Mom and Dad in the Old Orthodox cemetery in Millville. It took me a while to get over losing him so soon after we had finally found him. I had no regrets for spending a part of my life running his store but wished only that God had given us more time together as a family.

PART FOUR

The CIA Years

All statements of fact, opinion, or analysis expressed are those of the author and do not reflect the official positions or views of the Central Intelligence Agency (CIA) or any other U. S. Government agency. Nothing in the contents should be construed as asserting or implying U. S. Government authentication of information or CIA endorsement of the author's views. This material has been reviewed by the CIA to prevent the disclosure of classified information. This does not constitute an official release of CIA information.

Chapter 26

New Careers and Challenges in DC

We left Millville in 1983, never dreaming that we would end up in government work in the Washington, DC, area. Jerry applied to several federal agencies in Washington, but they all required a security background check, given his area of specialty—Russian. As prospective employers warned Jerry, in some cases it could take up to a year to get security clearances, which were likely to be complicated by my overseas birth. In the meantime, he searched the papers for an interim job but seemed to have little success.

I was cleaning up our home for eventual sale and happened to look at a Philadelphia newspaper's employment section; there, I found that Dover High School, in Dover, Delaware, was searching for a high school teacher qualified to teach German and French. I pointed it out to Jerry, and he half-heartedly applied for the advertised position, assuming the school would not be interested in him, based on previous application responses that he was overqualified for high school teaching. To his surprise, he was interviewed by phone and asked to come to Dover to interview in person. The interview went well, and he was offered the position with a good salary. Jerry came home, announcing that we were moving to Delaware.

Selling our house was not an easy task. Our good friend Lyuba had a real estate license, and we listed the house with her. Jerry's new position required that he begin teaching as the new school year started, so he found an apartment to rent in Dover, while I stayed behind to work on a job I had taken a year ago in the neighboring town of Vineland and to wait for a buyer for the house. Our children were both already in college—Nick at Carnegie Mellon and Chris at Bucknell, which made moving somewhat easier, except for my mom. Dad's death and Nick's disappearance had taken its toll on her, and the idea that we would be gone as well absolutely terrified her. At the same time, she insisted that she would not be relocated from her house. She wanted to be near the church and the cemetery where Dad was buried.

The announcement that Jerry had a job in Dover and we would be moving there angered her to the point of not wanting to have anything to do with either one of us. She refused to even let me come to visit her. I had suffered quite a bit with her anger at Dad's death, which she took out on me, as well as Nick's disappearance, and felt helpless to comfort her in any way. The best I could do was to pray that she recovered soon and would appreciate having had us near her for almost five years. We also pointed out that Dover was relatively near to Millville, and we would come to visit her often. Unfortunately, we had been unsuccessful in finding my brother Nick by that time, and Mom's reluctance to leave Millville was also tied to her hope that Nick would return soon.

Several months after Jerry started teaching at Dover, we sold our Millville house. Given the depressed real estate market in the area, we were lucky to come out even, without losing money on the sale. We found a lovely home to rent in Dover and had our goods moved there. I was hired by the State Historic Preservation Society in Dover soon after the move, and we began to make friends through the church we joined and to enjoy the more leisurely pace of Dover, glad to have the McCloskey Store experience behind us. We visited Mom often, once she accepted the need for us to move to continue with our careers.

As Jerry earned several promotions and was happy to be teaching languages again, we started to feel like this might become our permanent life style and began to think about buying the house we were renting from our landlords, who had become good friends and were ready to sell to us. But God had other plans for our lives, and before Jerry could accept another contract with the school, he received word that a job was waiting for him in Washington, DC, with the federal government. A government language school, Office of Training and Education, was prepared to hire him at a more lucrative salary and make use of the Slavic languages of which he was an expert. We agonized about leaving Dover and making the decision to move to the DC area, which we knew would be more hectic and challenging, but at the same time more satisfying professionally. We were also concerned about finding housing in the area, where real estate was much more expensive.

Jerry ended up accepting the position, however, and left for the DC area in the summer of 1984 to get an orientation for his new assignment and to find a place for us to live. I again stayed behind to pack our belongings and arrange for the move to McLean, Virginia, where Jerry found us a house to rent. Jerry had turned forty-nine in April of that year, and I was forty-five years old. Starting new careers at those ages seemed daunting, but we were both excited and challenged. Our kids were even more excited and teased Jerry about his reluctance to leave Dover. "How can you even compare the two places?" Nick asked him.

Finding a job for me was not as easy. I, too, applied to several federal agencies, but after filling out numerous pages of applications, came up with nothing. The cost of living in the Washington area and our bare years in Millville required me to find something. I ended up

applying to an electrical cooperative as administrative
assistant to the vice president and after passing typing
and shorthand tests, the latter in which I had no expertise but used my college shorthand, I was hired. The
office was in Georgetown and a challenge to drive to
from McLean, but my boss was excellent, and I spent
a happy year working there. Jerry, however, urged me
to follow up on my application to the CIA.

In checking on the application I had filled out for
the CIA, I found that it had been lost, according to the
personnel director, who advised me to fill out a new
one. It was hard for Jerry and me to imagine that the
agency could not take advantage of my native Russian
skills, so I once again filled out the lengthy form, especially since the agency would fulfill my desire to serve
the country in some capacity. Jerry advised me to apply
to the Foreign Broadcast Information Service (FBIS),
which published translations of foreign language news-
papers for scholars and government employees. He had
met one of its managers in a job fair his managers sent
him to with the goal of looking for applicants. The manager took an interest in me and my language skills, and
my application to FBIS was well received. I was called
in for an interview and subsequently hired.

The job opened a world of foreign politics, which
I found fascinating. I spent three years studying the
former Soviet Union and selecting pertinent articles
for translation, as well as managing language officers

in their selection of press articles. My career was moving upward, and I was quite happy with it and my work there.

On one occasion, I was asked to prepare a presentation to the CIA's Office of Intelligence Analysis and apparently provided new information that the analysts were seeking. A manager from that division approached me about joining his analytical team to write and provide briefings of current analysis on Soviet affairs for the president and for other high-level government officials. Just the idea of such a responsibility scared me speechless, but I managed to stammer out that I would like to consider the possibility. My application to the CIA was already in the works, and the fact that a special division was interested in my joining it, made the analyst position a reality. Before I knew it, I became a junior analyst, with all the challenges inherent in the position.

Chapter 27

On the Ground in the Soviet Union

My experience as an English and Slavic litera-ture major in college and graduate school at Columbia did not prepare me for the writing I had to do as an analyst. Analytic writing has a style of its own, with the "bottom line up front," starting with the conclusion and proceeding to argue and prove one's point from there. It consists of a tightly knit analytical essay of two to three pages, which gives the president and his cabinet a succinct description of what is hap-pening with an international political event, why it is important to write about it or its impact, where the sit-uation is heading, and what can be done to mitigate the harm it could cause if some action is not taken. Easily said, but hard to accomplish in such a short space, and the numerous layers of review the piece faces makes it that much more difficult. Not knowing its structure and organization, I found it an agony to put together a piece in the space of two to three hours and send it forward for others to critique—and to defend its final form, once critiqued. If not for a patient and extremely competent manager, who guided me through the pitfalls, I would probably have quit the job.

I managed to muddle through my first few years as an analyst, and it wasn't until the third year that I finally felt comfortable being one. Since very little information came from behind the Iron Curtain, finding topics to write about was a challenge and making them relevant and interesting an even greater one. I was anxious to "be on the ground" and to talk to the Soviet people—to find out what they were thinking and how they reacted to their isolation from the rest of the world.

I met State Department colleagues and envied their being stationed abroad and began to look at possibilities of joining them for "on the ground" experience. My first chance came as our government signed the Intermediate Ballistic Missile Treaty (INF), with the Soviet Union to reduce the number of nuclear missiles each country possessed. The State Department began to search for competent Russian speakers who could interpret for American missile inspectors in the Soviet Union. I took a leave of absence from my CIA unit when my application to become an interpreter for INF was accepted and left for Germany shortly thereafter. Our inspectors traveled from Germany to various parts of the Soviet Union once an agreement was reached on the destination. From Moscow, they were bussed to various missile sites for inspecting or counting the number of missiles on that site. Once a report was prepared, they returned to Germany to wait for the next trip.

Being in the Soviet Union since I left Latvia so many years ago was an experience I will never forget. The Russian and Ukrainian countryside, with its decorated wooden houses and white fences, was beautiful and reminded me of pictures I had seen on record covers of Russian folk song albums. Stately birch trees lined the sides of the road and grew wildly in the lush woods surrounding the villages, reminding me of the aspens of Utah and the American West. Small garden plots with the rich, black soil of the Ukraine were located by railroad tracks and in areas one would not expect to see them. Old Babushkas with their multi-flowered scarfs and embroidered long skirts walking along the road or milking an occasional cow made me smile and wave in greeting. It was like a wonderland that one expected to see in an old Soviet movie, but still very much alive and well. A train trip to the Russian Far East made me feel like I was a part of the movie *Dr. Zhivago,* as we bounced along the winding railroad tracks. The music of Lara's theme kept swirling in my head, and I felt a joy in my heart to be in this country I and my family had to leave behind many years ago.

On one of our inspection trips I was joined by two Russian officers' wives, who had learned that I spoke their language. The Russians were not expecting females to be a part of the inspection team, and when I and another military interpreter appeared, they quickly summoned officers' wives to accompany us. They walked alongside our group, dressed in thin summer dresses with their arms exposed to the myriad of mosquitos mercilessly landing on their bare flesh and with high heels sinking into the mud of the paths we were taking, chattering incessantly and asking numerous questions about Americans and their way of life. One surprised me by saying, "Oh, but you don't look like one!"

"One what?" I asked, puzzled by her exclamation.

"Like a prostitute," she responded. "We were told that most American women are prostitutes, but you seem pretty normal to us." The statement shocked me until I realized that we were still in a Cold War situation and these women had grown up studying and believing Marxist philosophy and teachings that Western civilizations were basically corrupt and immoral.

"Believe me, I'm a mother of two children and about to become a grandmother. What a strange thing for you to say! American women are hard-working and certainly not prostitutes," I said, laughing heartily, and wondering if my slacks and long-sleeved blouse and boots to protect from snakes and mosquitos looked out of place, compared to the two of them and their fancy outfits. I silently handed one a mosquito spray can and pointed to her arm, turning red from mosquito bites. "Spray it on," I said. "It will protect you."

I spent almost two months interpreting for inspectors, despite agreeing to go for only two weeks. Two subsequent trips, shorter in duration, to watch these missiles be blown to shreds were equally historic and gave me much comfort to know that they could no longer threaten the world with their awesome power of nuclear destruction.

Jerry was beginning to think he would never see me again, and our occasional phone calls did little to keep him from becoming lonely and anxious to have me at home. Despite the guilt I felt for being away so long, I would not have changed a day in that exciting experience of being on Russian and Ukrainian soil and using the language of my ancestors to communicate. I came back home convinced that I needed to go again—and soon.

Chapter 28

The Soviet Union Disintegrates

M y next exciting trip to the Soviet Union came in 1991, when I was sent to Leningrad, which was renamed St. Petersburg shortly after the break-up of the Soviet Union. As a Slavic analyst, I had been watching for signs of weakening of the Soviet regime and was fortunate enough to witness its downfall on the ground in St. Petersburg.

The city was well laid out, and I found it fascinating to roam the streets of Leningrad, with buildings rich in historically beautiful architecture and picturesque bridges, and to visit its famous museums on weekends. I was in my element, increasing my Russian proficiency and enjoying the beautiful winter days that brought out the populace and allowed me to chat with the elderly and college students lounging in the city's many parks. I wandered in and out of residential areas, admiring the architecture and the color of apartment buildings— most in lovely pastels but in need of critical repair. The Soviet system was not kind to the famous city's infrastructure, and the lack of privatization kept buildings in disrepair.

Two college students struck up a conversation with me soon after I arrived, and I was fortunate that they took an interest in an American who spoke decent Russian. They were studying at the St. Petersburg School of Economics, a prestigious university that mentored the children of well-connected parents, and I later realized that one of my student friends, Medvedev, may have become the prime minister of Russia, taking over after President Putin's first tenure. On one occasion, I also unknowingly met the future president of Russia—Putin himself—when I was introduced to him in the economics building, but he did not seem too pleased to make my acquaintance, excusing himself quickly after the initial greetings.

My two Russian acquaintances were the opposite, anxious to discuss American ways of life, particularly in universities, and they saw to it that I became thoroughly acquainted with Leningrad and all it had to offer. They expressed their sincere regrets when it was time for me to leave and surprised me with a gift of a velvet flag that held pins representing major events and places in the Soviet Union, which Medvedev had collected throughout his school years.

Politically, the country was beginning to feel the years of Soviet rule, and I could sense that the government, under President Gorbachev, was experiencing turmoil. I had brought my portable radio with me and listened to Russian news stations nightly, sensing that something was about to break.

An important Soviet Politburo meeting took place the night before the break-up, and I listened closely to the news commentaries on the event, certain that I would hear something as a result of the meeting that went far into the night. I went to bed tired but restless, and woke up early in the morning to see if anything had transpired that night. Tuning into my radio, I was surprised to hear only classical music and changed stations to see if others had some news. All had classical music, and I suddenly realized that there must have been a government coup that took place during the night. Classical music was historically a sign of government turnover in the Soviet Union.

"I knew it; I knew it," I said to myself in excitement, and quickly showered and dressed. It was still very early in the morning when I finished, but I again went to my radio, this time to hear the announcer talk about the government coup and fighting in the streets of Moscow, with Yeltsin declaring the independence of Russia and the fall of the Soviet government. I could hardly contain my excitement as I listened to the details of Yeltsin on the tank, declaring himself the president of Russia and the battles of freedom fighters in the streets of Moscow.

I heard a knock on the door, and a voice asking if I was awake. My driver wanted to know if I was aware of what had happened during the night, and I pointed to my radio, which was still providing news of the coup.

"I've been awake all night working," he told me. "You need to get to work to find out what is happening in Leningrad. I'll walk you there since we may be in danger, after you pack a small bag with your valuables in case we need to be evacuated today. It might be dangerous for us to remain here."

I welcomed his offer to walk me there but wondered why he wasn't planning to drive, especially if he felt it was dangerous for us to be downtown. Walking would certainly make us more vulnerable, but I didn't question his judgment. I took my small duffle bag already prepared for a quick getaway and stuffed my portable radio inside. Grabbing it and my purse, I followed him outside.

The streets were quiet, considering the activity going on in Moscow, but I suspected Leningrad residents were probably glued to their radios and felt that staying home was the safest alternative. We arrived at work without incident.

Since Leningrad was the second seat of government, so to speak, it was logical that the expelled communist leaders might try to wrest power from Moscow by bringing forces loyal to them and taking over Leningrad.

I started to listen to the local station on my radio and soon the announcer began to describe the local situation. Apparently, the toppled communist leaders had in fact decided to take over Leningrad and had sent their troops, a contingent of which had a base outside of Leningrad, to the city gates. The city was fortunate in its choice of mayors, with a liberal/democratic mayor who had been in close contact with the US government after his election.

Mayor Sobachak, when he learned about the troops coming to his city, mobilized the Soviet Air Force, housed within the city's central square and loyal to the mayor, to meet and challenge the communist troops at the gate. The air force won the battle and the opposition forces scattered, saving the city. Mayor Sobachak declared that Leningrad would from now on be called by its historic name, St. Petersburg, and invited its citizens to gather in St Isaac's Square that afternoon to bring them up to date on the latest events.

I set out for the square after lunch, and as I began to walk, I heard a strange noise around me, like the "clip clopping" of horses' feet. This turned out to be the sound of numerous residents of Leningrad coming from every corner of every street and all heading for St. Isaac's, their shoes echoing with the strange sound as they all walked along. I arrived at St. Isaac's Square to see it filling up with people, all facing the large scaffolding erected to hold the mayor and his entourage.

Loudspeakers were set up on the scaffolding, and music was blasting from the loudspeakers, playing the Russian national anthem. Hanging from the scaffolding was a huge tri-colored red, white, and blue Russian flag.

I inched toward the front of the huge crowd, now standing shoulder to shoulder, and asked my neighbors what they expected to hear from the mayor and what was happening around the city. "We have our own heroes in Leningrad," they told me. "They have been fighting at the gates, toppling statues of Stalin and other communist leaders and taking over the TV and radio stations," they explained proudly.

The music stopped as the popular mayor and his cohorts stepped to the front of the scaffolding. A thunderous shout went up from the huge square, filled with the city's residents standing shoulder to shoulder and clapping loudly. Women were wiping their eyes as the mayor began to describe the situation at the gates of St. Petersburg, as he called it.

"These air force soldiers are our heroes," the Mayor said proudly and pointed to a tall building housing the air force nearby. As another deafening shout went up, windows opened in the building and a huge Russian flag was lowered out of the windows against the wall of the building. Loud clapping ensued for what seemed like at least ten minutes until the mayor stilled the crowd.

"Let's have a moment of silence for our heroes who died in Moscow, defending our freedom," the mayor told the crowd, as they all bowed their heads. He then explained to them what to expect in the next several days, and once he finished, the music began to play once again. People congratulated each other, some hugging while others shaking hands. Several Russians came over to me and shook my hand, one telling me that Russia will be great again and become good friends with America. I stood there, nodding my head and thinking about this historic moment, never to be duplicated and how blessed I was to witness it all.

I left with the crowd, all quietly moving to their streets and making the same "clip clopping" sound as thousands of feet went home to a different world than they had been used to and probably wondering what was ahead of them.

I had a ticket to fly to Kiev, Ukraine, and was anxious to get there since I knew the country was also debating its future.

Chapter 29

Ukraine Earns Independence

M y trip from Moscow to Ukraine was difficult to arrange, although I already had a ticket to fly to Kiev. The Soviet airlines were in chaos, and passengers who had tickets found that they were practically useless. People boarded the plane with tickets they had just purchased, forcing out those who had arranged for them earlier. My ticket was not recognized by the airlines, and it wasn't until I insisted on seeing the "man in charge" of Aeroflot airlines at the time and convinced him that the US President expected me to use the issued ticket to get to Kiev or he would have to answer to the US that he stamped my ticket with a first-class confirmation that I could use to board the plane. I squeezed into a seat that was empty in the front and refused to move—regardless of who tried to force me out, flashing a US passport and speaking only in English. I arrived in Kiev and was met by a middle-aged man called John, who welcomed me, and took me to the hotel he had arranged for me to stay in.

Since Russia and Ukraine had a long history of unity, and Kiev was considered by Russians to be the heart of the Orthodox faith, the Western Ukrainians, mostly Russian speakers, were unwilling to have the country separate from its parent. Eastern Ukrainians, however, with their center in Lvov, spoke Ukrainian and were fierce nationalists who wanted to take advantage of this historic occasion to free Ukraine from Russia. A legislative session was to be held the following day to decide on Ukraine's fate, and authorities in Kiev were apparently expecting some problems with the spectators who wanted a free Ukraine. There were rumors of possible riots and disturbances.

I arrived early the next morning in the square that was in front of the capital building and sat down on a park bench adjoining the area. As I looked toward the building, I saw that there was a cordon of militia officers guarding its entrance, standing quietly in front of the steps to the building.

I was soon joined by a young man who looked like a college student, and I could see that he wanted to engage me in a conversation on what was about to occur. I introduced myself, speaking the Ukrainian that I learned in a summer in Harvard, and was relieved that he was an excellent Russian speaker who knew some English as well. We conversed freely in Russian, and he explained to me that the area around the building was wired for sound, and the entire session of the legislature would be heard outside.

Crowds began to gather in front of the building, and we could hear the preparation for the loudspeakers to be engaged. The student took me by the wrist and propelled us both to the front of the building, directly in front of the militia members, cordoning off the entrance. On either side of the steps were statues of Ukrainian heroes who prevented entrance to the building, and militia guards stood by their side. The militia thus formed a fence around the front steps, so people could not enter freely into the capital building.

The session began shortly thereafter, and as I looked around, I could see that the square had filled with bystanders standing shoulder to shoulder, listening to the sounds coming out of the loudspeakers. As President Kravchuk began to speak, the crowd let out a loud shout, and some of the braver ones began to push in on the militia members, now standing with their guns outstretched. We were right in the front, and I could see the discomfort on the faces of the militia as people began to try to get around them and climb the stairs of the building. Some braver ones were climbing on the statues standing by the sides of the stairs, and militia members were pointing their guns toward them. The crowd had suddenly become unruly, and I began to wonder if I should move back from the force of the crowd pushing us forward toward the militia, who I could tell were prepared to fire if necessary.

Just as the crowd became more unruly, unhappy with what was progressing inside and over the loudspeakers, the doors of the capital swung open, and a leader of the Rukh faction came out. Rukh was the Ukrainian independent party lobbying for a free Ukraine. He was holding a loudspeaker in his hands. The curious crowd stopped shoving and began to listen to his voice.

"Let's have a moment of silence for the citizens who died defending the capital in Moscow and freeing people from the oppression of the communists," he said loudly. The crowd stilled and stood quietly for at least three minutes. Just as it became restless again, the doors of the capital swung open once more, and women dressed in Ukrainian native costumes appeared on the top steps of the building and began to sing the Orthodox funeral dirge. The crowd joined in and the tension of the moment disappeared. The Rukh leader then urged the crowd to have patience and listen to the debate going inside. He reassured them that the outcome would be a good one for Ukraine and that it would become an independent country, free from the yoke of Russia. This seemed to satisfy the crowd, and people began to mill around, while listening to the voices inside. Each time they heard something that displeased them, they again began to shout and move toward the building but stopped short of trying to climb over the militia, holding its position. I could see legislators peering out of the windows to watch the crowd's reaction to the session going on inside.

The legislative session continued well into the afternoon, and the scene repeated itself. As the debate inside got more intense, the crowd outside reacted accordingly, and calmer voices of the legislators seemed to prevail and silence the crowd. "It will take some time," the Ukrainian student told me confidently, "but I think that Kravchuk will vote for independence before the day is over. It's obvious that he is influenced by the crowd's reactions outside," he concluded.

By the end of the afternoon, I had to return to prepare for my flight back. Since my ticket to St. Petersburg was for that evening, I reluctantly left to get to the airport, and once there, listened intently to the many television screens in the airport to see what the results of the session had been. By five that afternoon, and before my flight arrived, President Kravchuk announced that he was in favor of a free Ukraine and was draped by his lawmakers with the Ukrainian national flag. Ukrainians in the airport cheered loudly and congratulated each other on their new independent country, relieved that their president had sided with them.

I scurried outside, having heard my plane for St. Petersburg being announced, and found myself pushing crowds on the tarmac to get inside the plane. On entering the plane, I found it completely occupied and wondered how I would get out of Ukraine before my visa expired. Just as I was about to deplane, I heard a woman in the back of the plane calling me to join her. "Little sister," she said. "There's a seat left for you here at the very end of the plane. Hurry and get in here, or you'll end up losing it." I happily ran to the back and inched toward the only empty seat left in the entire plane. "And don't move out of the seat, even if Kravchuk himself tells you he wants that seat," the old woman added as I pushed past her to the window seat. There was no way anyone could dislodge me at that point, and I arrived safely back in St. Petersburg, only to board a plane back to the US the next day.

Chapter 30

A Historic Trip to Moscow

R eturning to the States after the excitement I experienced in the former Soviet Union would have
been a let-down, except for the overwhelmingly busy
period we had at the agency after the break-up of the
Soviet Union. I began to monitor the events there,
especially since most of the Soviet Union's strategic
missiles were stored in the Ukraine, now an independent country. Kiev did not have the power to launch or
operate the missiles, Russia did, but the fact that they
were housed on their soil gave the Ukrainians a certain
amount of leverage and power. They steadfastly refused
to turn them over to Moscow, at Russia's urging, and
the United States became the arbiter in trying to convince Kiev to do just that. As analysts, we were all kept
busy, informing the president and the National Security
Council regarding this situation.

I had authored a lengthy inter-agency study draft
of this entire situation, which was then reviewed by
all the intelligence agencies, ending up looking quite

different from my original draft. Intellectually, these were exciting times for me and kept me happy at my desk. However, an unexpected longer trip came up when the director of Central Intelligence's chief interpreter became ill on a planned trip to Russia and Ukraine, and I was asked to serve as the DCI's interpreter in Russia. Terrified, I tried to dodge this assignment, pointing out that my Russian, while decent, did not come up to the level of a professional interpreter's, nor did I have many opportunities to practice it lately.

My superiors would not accept this as an excuse, since the trip was a "first" historically, and I finally agreed with the understanding that I would be the DCI's social interpreter primarily and would correct any errors I heard come from the many well-trained Russian interpreters during our meetings and technical discussions. The DCI, of course, was never informed of my limitations, nor did he know that I was one of his analysts and not a professional interpreter. This put me in an awkward position from the start. I flew to Moscow and met his Air Force One plane as he landed with his team, and from the start found myself interpreting for the greeting session as well as other events as they occurred. I was able to perform for them to the DCI's satisfaction.

It wasn't until a critical technical meeting took place on the second day that I showed my limitations as an interpreter, to my dismay. To this day, I believe the Russians set me up, curious to see who I really was. The DCI's host, Yevgeniy Primakov, spoke English quite well, having served at the UN as an ambassador, but the rest of his staff expected the session to be in Russian. Their interpreter met me as I was coming to the meeting and introduced himself, chatting while we waited outside.

"Which is easier for you, to interpret from Russian into English or English into Russian?" he asked at one point.

"From Russian into English," I replied. "Since I'm primarily an English speaker."

"The same is true for me," he answered. "Going from English into Russian is a lot easier for me, than the other way around."

I wondered why he had asked me that, since it was my understanding that he would be doing most of the interpreting, having studied the art for at least ten years. This was the technical meeting I was dreading, and I had reminded my American hosts of my limitations when I arrived. I walked into the meeting, feeling quite anxious as I sat down next to the DCI. His counterpart Primakov was seated at the other side of the table with his interpreter.

As the meeting began, Mr. Primakov began to welcome the guests in Russian, and as he did so, his interpreter pointed to me and said, "Please start." Although in shock from what was happening, I began to interpret

Mr. Primakov's greeting, straining to hear his nasal and quiet Russian. I did well enough until the man began to launch into technical issues, never stopping or pausing for me to gather the meaning, as is customary with such bilingual events. Primakov just continued to speak while I strained to listen and interpret on the fly, eventually losing his thread, as he continued to drone on in his nasal tones.

"Excuse me, sir" I said quietly, interrupting him. "Did you want simultaneous interpretation?"

Primakov winked at me and half-smiled. "I thought in the interest of efficiency, we would do simultaneous," he responded.

"I'm sorry, sir," I stuttered. "I don't do simultaneous. We'll just have to let your interpreter do that."

"Of course," Primakov said without losing a beat, as if he expected it in the first place, and continued to drone on. As his interpreter began to show his skill in keeping up with the man, Primakov stopped him abruptly and said in English, "That's not what I said," and interpreted for himself on the particular point he was making. He then stopped and told his interpreter, "Go on," continuing his monotonous speech, while the interpreter, sweating profusely, tried to keep up with him. Primakov's entire speech became a confusing jumble of English as spoken by his interpreter, and I had to whisper in the DCI's ears several times when he turned to me questioningly when the English interpretation did not make sense.

I was mortified, especially when I sensed that the DCI was displeased with my lack of ability to interpret Primakov simultaneously. People who don't study foreign languages assume all interpreting is the same. He was understandably embarrassed, and I just wanted to crawl under the table. I stubbornly refused to interpret into Russian when it was the DCI's turn to speak, and pointed to Primakov's interpreter, "Please begin." Fortunately for him, the DCI paused to allow him to interpret before continuing, probably because he wanted to make sure he was understood correctly. I could not wait for the meeting to finish, so I could go hide somewhere, preferably in my hotel room.

Since this was just the beginning of many more technical meetings, I made sure that the DCI knew where I was coming from and that I had been asked to interpret primarily for social venues. Once he learned of my position, the DCI became much more understanding, and we ended the Moscow part of the trip amicably, as we set off for St. Petersburg, flying in the "Kennedy" Air Force One.

Our arrival in St. Petersburg was greeted with a Russian band playing "As the Saints Go Marching In," which made the DCI declare that his trip was worthy of the effort and one he would not easily forget. Our time there was less stressful, as the many anxious Russian interpreters took their turns at interpreting during the technical sessions.

The planned trip also included a stop in Ukraine, to deal with the matter of Russian missiles on their soil. As he prepared to continue to Ukraine, the DCI asked if I knew Ukrainian and would be coming along. "I was just asked for the Russian part of the trip," I explained to him. The DCI had learned about my background on the Ukraine issue and the piece I had written for inter-agency discussion, and insisted that I go with him to Kiev, briefing him on the way regarding the situation in Ukraine. I agreed to accompany him on Air Force One but warned him that my Ukrainian was limited, and I would most certainly not be able to do simultaneous interpretation in Ukrainian. The DCI laughed and said, "But they all speak Russian anyway, so you'll be in good shape." How right he turned out to be!

When we arrived in Ukraine, the DCI's host greeted us in Ukrainian, and I had to interpret for the two of them in Ukrainian until we moved to the technical meetings. When the first meeting began, the speaker noted that "Mrs. Liston is primarily a Russian interpreter, so we'll hold the sessions in Russian." I had to chuckle, since I knew that most of the attendees were Russian-speaking and probably could not handle a meeting in Ukrainian, even if they tried. I was a good excuse to save face for them.

The trip with the DCI turned out to be a successful one, and he was pleased with the outcome. I had been under such stress during the entire time that I developed a bad cold and was truly happy when it all ended. My only problem was that since I came with the DCI on Air Force One to Ukraine and was not planning to do so, I did not have a visa for that country. When the DCI was leaving and complaining to me about having to go back to the States rather than further on his planned trip, I admitted that he was luckier than I. "At least you have a ride home. I may be stuck in Kiev for a long time," I told him. Once he realized that I did not have a ticket home or a visa for Ukraine, he quickly invited me to join him on Air Force One.

Chapter 31

Developing Contacts in Moscow

T he trip with the Director of Central Intelligence convinced me that I needed to spend more time in Russia to bring my Russian to a native level. I also witnessed the stress my husband was under in his job and wanted to get him away from the States, especially since he was eligible for retirement in two years. I explored possibilities for a longer assignment in Russia and found that only the State Department had extended assignments to Moscow. In 1995, an opportunity opened for analysts to compete for two-year assignments in Moscow with the State Department. I applied in hopes of getting a long-term assignment by transferring to the State Department.

My career at CIA seemed to be at a standstill. My superiors were talking to me about possible management positions, but these were few and far between, and it was hard to know when and if a position would materialize. My boss did not seem anxious for me to apply to State and go abroad. His mind-set was one of "out of sight, out of mind," and I felt like I was jeopardizing my future career if the job at State did not come through. I applied anyway and, by some miracle, got the assignment.

Competition for the slot with State was challenging. I had learned that a young analyst was in line for the job, approved by his supervisors and favored by the selection committee, and it looked like I had little chance for the assignment. Luckily, he pulled out of the competition, concerned that his Russian proficiency was limited, leaving me the only applicant.

Jerry was delighted to learn that we would be going to Moscow. He took a leave of absence from his job and prepared meticulously for the trip. Both of us were excited by the prospect of being there to witness the country's efforts to become democratic under President Yeltsin's regime. A professor friend from Texas who had escaped the Soviet Union and settled in the States was planning to visit Moscow. When he learned about our upcoming assignment there, he told us that he hoped to look up his university friends in Moscow and would introduce us to them.

"It's hard to break into Russian society unless you have a friend or a mentor who gets you in," he told us. "My introductions will give you a good start while there." He kept his promise, which opened doors for us to many Russians we would not have been able to meet on our own.

Since we were newcomers to the Embassy, I was assigned to the Embassy's condominium apartment complex called Rosinka. It was a State Department development in the far reaches of Moscow that contained American-style apartments that many State department officers preferred to the Russian ones, when they could not get an apartment in the Embassy compound. The disadvantage to these apartments was the long bus ride to reach them. The Embassy had a schedule of buses that transported its staff to these apartments, but the buses stopped at 7 p.m.

Because I was one of the better Russian speakers, I was often assigned to escort official US delegations (we called them CODELS), consisting mostly of congressmen and -women and to set up appointments for them with Russian officials they wished to interview. These meetings often lasted past 7 p.m., and I found myself stranded at the Embassy without bus transportation home to Rosinka, often late in the evening.

It was especially frustrating, since it took at least three months to receive our automobiles from the States, and I found myself having to take the metro to the end of the line, wait by a bus station for at least forty-five minutes, crowd into an overfilled bus heading to the countryside, and be dropped off five miles from the Rosinka complex, to walk a deserted road in the dark for five miles to get home. After my first frightening walk home, with strange cars stopping to offer me a ride, I arranged with Jerry to have him meet me by the bus drop off, calculating when I might get there. Unfortunately, Jerry often came too early or too late, walking the five-mile distance and waiting for me to appear since we could not communicate when I got close to the bus drop off.

Changing our assigned place of residence took concerted effort on the part of my supervisor, who had to write a request to the State residence assignment committee and to send his most qualified and convincing representative to argue my case for an apartment in the city of Moscow rather than in Rosinka. This did not occur until I simply refused to stay on the compound past 7 p.m., when the last bus departed for Rosinka. Shortly thereafter, we were reassigned to an apartment in the heart of Moscow, making it feasible to get to the Embassy by metro. Most importantly, this allowed us to invite Muscovites to our apartment in order to socialize with them, as my supervisor encouraged me to do. He often bragged afterward that I had developed contacts that were even more numerous than his. He found he could always call me when a law was passed that made little sense to have me question my contacts for its reason and meaning.

Our first big evening in our Moscow apartment with the Russians occurred after our professor friend flew to Moscow and arranged for a number of his friends, some of whom were politicians, artists, singers, theologians, and poets, to come to our house in order to experience a true American Thanksgiving dinner. Through the Embassy, I was able to order American food, including a twenty-pound turkey with all the trimmings, and we had dressing, cranberry sauce, sweet potatoes, and even pumpkin pie with ice cream for dessert. Our twenty-plus guests enjoyed the evening thoroughly, especially since Jerry and I were both fluent in Russian, making them feel comfortable to have lively conversations about any number of topics. That evening began a series of dinners at least once a month and brought many additional guests as they in turn introduced us to their friends and acquaintances.

One of the more interesting evenings we had with acquaintances whom we met through our wide group of friends was a Russian legislator, who we found out was responsible for drafting the strict law on religion that the Duma (Russian legislature) adopted and President Yeltsin refused to sign when it first appeared on his desk. Yeltsin could have been influenced to reject the law initially following the Embassy's discussion with the Russians on its ramifications. I briefed Ambassador Pickering on the law and its consequences for our American pastors, and back-benched him at the meeting with Yeltsin's chief representative Chubais. Ambassador Pickering presented a good argument against signing the law into effect, and Chubais may have advised the president to hold off on it.

The law would have prevented any other religion besides the Orthodox to be proselytized lawfully in Russia except for the religions that had traditionally been in existence in the country, such as Catholicism, Mormonism, and Assemblies of God—churches which had been established years ago and enjoyed a limited following in Russia. Even these churches were in danger of being restricted in where and how they could function. No new church starts would have been allowed, even with the traditional religions above. Unfortunately, the second time the law was brought before the legislature and President Yeltsin, he was pressured to sign it into effect.

During one dinner after the law was first rejected by Yeltsin, Jerry and I learned that one of our guests had been responsible for drafting the law and bringing it before the legislature. Jerry asked the legislator what prompted him to draft the law. He explained to Jerry that when the Soviet Union fell apart, Russian Orthodox believers thought that Americans would come to their aid in rebuilding the churches that were destroyed during communism and Stalin's reign. Instead, the Americans sent their pastors and missionaries to proselytize their own religions, many of which attracted Russian youth and turned them away from their Orthodox roots.

"But that's freedom of religion," Jerry told the legislator. "It's one of the guiding principles in our country."

"Not in ours," the legislator responded. "We believe in keeping our own faith in our country, and refusing to let others impinge on it, legally or illegally. If Americans don't support us, they and their religions are not welcome here," he concluded.

"So, it's like the old Communist principle: If I don't have a cow and my neighbor does, his will have to be killed," I piped in somewhat angrily.

This did not sit well with the Russian, and he and I got into a polemic on religion. Our friend the theologian sensed that I was on dangerous ground in challenging the legislator and quickly began to diffuse the conversation. He had brought the legislator as his guest and did not want to suffer the consequences of his anger, nor did he want Jerry and me to be on the wrong side of powerful people in Russia.

We ended the evening cordially, and I hoped that I did not overstep my bounds in being a difficult hostess. I had certainly learned a good lesson in challenging Russians, especially powerful ones, at the dinner table. Fortunately for us, the legislator liked Jerry and invited him to come visit him in his office at the Kremlin. They became friends, and I was forgiven. Later, when the strict law on religion was brought up again and passed, I wondered if I had been in any way responsible for its reemergence.

Our theologian friend got himself in trouble with the Orthodox after we left Russia, I learned later. He had a TV show on Russian television in which he was asked questions that had to do with Russian Orthodoxy and answered them for his audience. One day when he came to do his show, a Russian had sent in a question on a celebration that had taken place the week before for the Orthodox Patriarch's birthday—a lively event with many high-level officials and TV stars, the rich and the famous—asking if it was appropriate for the Patriarch to have such an elaborate celebration. The theologian had responded honestly and carefully. Since the Patriarch's name was changed when he was ordained, said the theologian, he theoretically no longer had the birthday to celebrate.

The following week when the theologian came to the studio for his show, he was told that he no longer had the job and was not welcome in the studio. Depressed and considerably poorer with the loss of his income and a job he enjoyed, he retired to a small country house, where he spent the rest of his days writing and reading in solitude—such a loss for the country of a man who wrote brilliant essays and poetry. He admired Jerry and wrote a special poem for his birthday, using partly Russian and partly English. He was one of the more colorful Russians we had the pleasure to know.

Chapter 32

Saved by the Fire Extinguisher

We found Moscow quite dangerous at times but managed to stay alive and well throughout my two-year assignment. The Russia we faced was struggling in 1996 to survive the breakup of the Soviet Union five years back and to become a different, more modern and democratic country. President Yeltsin, however, missed his chance to make it happen by falling back on his communist friends and old habits. Discontent with the system was brewing, and a backlash of unhappiness with Americans who were trying to turn the country around was quite evident in our daily lives there.

One day, as I was talking on the phone with Jerry at my work station in the old Embassy building, I heard a loud crash below our floor. "I've got to go, honey," I told him as I ran to the window to see what had happened, being told later that it was exactly the wrong thing to do under the circumstances. I got to the window in time to see a man in a black hood hurrying away from across the street, with what looked like a weapon under his arm. He had just let a small missile (RPG) sail into the floor below us, which exploded against a Xerox duplication machine standing there. I saw him get into a car and quickly drive away. The Russian authorities were unable to determine who the perpetrator had been but guessed that it might have been a disgruntled KGB employee.

Consular officers did not enjoy taking turns on staffing the front window where Russians picked up and returned forms for visas to the US and being asked questions about qualifications and waiting times, since the Russians were often dissatisfied for one reason or another and tended to be rude and overbearing. One lady even smacked the front bullet-proof window with her heavy purse and broke it. The bullet proofing of the windows continued into the entrance where Russians came to be interviewed and stopped at a counter where they left their bags and cameras and other items they carried. A consular officer sat by the front window and was flanked by a US security guard for protection. That officer found himself in a life-threatening situation one day. A middle-aged Russian woman dressed in a beautiful fur coat entered the lobby area of the Consulate and asked a guard standing in the hall if she could make a call to a diplomat whose card she flashed. "The phone is behind me on the wall," the guard pointed.

Instead of going to the phone, she walked behind the guard and poured something on his back. The guard quickly turned around as he smelled gasoline and saw the woman light her cigarette lighter and bring it toward him. The frightened guard ducked and scampered away toward the back door.

The woman did not hesitate for a second. She took a bottle of gasoline out of her bag, poured it over the counter behind the officer and the guard, and set it on fire. Flames shot up quickly and trapped both men against the front bullet-proof window which also blocked off the side. They both ducked down as the flames came toward them, thinking they would be engulfed. The officer looked up as he felt something wet coming down on him and was hit in the eyes with the liquid. Thinking it was more gasoline, he crouched lower. Fortunately for both of them, it was the Embassy sprinkling system, pouring out chemicals to douse the flames. The flames disappeared, but clouds of dense smoke threatened to choke both victims. The officer told the guard to move toward the door, and when he realized the guard was paralyzed with fear, he literally picked him up and pushed him out the back entrance.

Fire alarms went off in the Embassy, and everyone began to evacuate. I was the fire marshal on our floor and quickly barked orders for everyone to go down the winding wrought-iron staircase to the back entrance. Unfortunately, I had surgery on my right foot several weeks prior and a cast almost up to my knee, making it difficult to climb stairs. Abandoning my crutch, I moved toward the stairway and was met by a young colleague who refused to run down ahead of me and instead helped me down the stairs slowly. Outside, people were milling around, trying to find out what had happened.

The Embassy was unable to learn who started the fire. The lady in the fur coat disappeared into the crowd during the excitement that ensued, with people being evacuated from the Consulate as the flames began to spread. Fortunately, the fire extinguishers worked to quell the flames and no one was injured. A woman called the next day and claimed she had set the fire, but when she agreed to come to the Embassy to discuss her actions, the guard who was approached by the original criminal fire-setter dismissed the volunteer who confessed to the fire as being much too old to have perpetrated the action.

Chapter 33

Invaded by the Militia

J erry and I enjoyed exploring Moscow and all it had
to offer. We attended the city's theaters, including
the famous Bolshoi and its marvelous ballets and
operas, and were introduced to the less well-known theater center, where young artists exhibited their art, some
of whom were friends of our newly-met acquaintances.
Jerry even started up a conversation with a wrestling
coach he met at one of the Embassy's receptions, who
was also a prolific writer, publishing in numerous countries. The writer invited him to a wrestling match—he
had at one time coached the famous Cuban wrestling
team into an international championship—to see the
art as it was performed in Moscow. He claimed Jerry
was an American correspondent, which got him into
the stadium, and introduced him to some "greats" in
the art of wrestling. He was so pleased with my husband that he invited us to his house for a gathering of
friends, something that was rare with the others we met
at the Thanksgiving dinner, probably because they were

embarrassed by their modest apartments, compared to the spacious one we had in the heart of the city. Jerry's new-found friend had a large apartment in Moscow that the Soviet government had given him for his wrestling achievements.

Jerry's wrestling coach-turned-writer also insisted that we come to the annual banquet for Russian writers, a lavish affair, and when he was told that Americans were not welcome, refused to attend unless the ban was lifted for his "good American friend Jerry." The writer's union relented, and we were the only Americans in attendance at their year-end banquet. Jerry's friend even made a special toast to his "distinguished American military officer (Jerry) who served bravely for his country." It was an evening to remember.

We started a round of dinners once a month, gathering new Russians from all walks of life, based on the Thanksgiving dinner that was such a success. Those in attendance brought their friends and acquaintances, and we often had twenty people at our dinner table. I prepared and served a full-course meal, beginning with snacks, followed by Russian soups such as borshcht, then a main course with meat, and ending with a dessert and after-dinner liqueurs. Once we finished the main course, the Russians relaxed and exhibited their many talents—some were well-known balladeers, some writers, some artists, and some politicians who regaled us with the current politics of the Kremlin. I was amazed when the quiet wife of a well-known artist turned out to be an excellent poetess. She produced a tiny notebook one evening when pressed by other guests and read some of the most beautiful poetry I had heard in a while. The evenings lasted well into the night, broken up only by the metro's last run, which many took to our house and back home.

These evenings aroused the attention of the Kremlin, and we began to be watched more carefully and monitored through eavesdropping by security officers who stationed themselves in the attic of our apartment. We were aware of their location and listening apparatus and were always careful about our own conversations. We even "talked to the walls" when they interfered with our telephone conversations to the US—closing down our connections to the States—and made it clear that we had to chat with our children and elderly mother, whose birthday had to be celebrated.

In one unforgettable incident, we found ourselves closely monitored when sponsoring a Bible class at our apartment that was requested by the Russian pastor of our church. He had rehabilitated a group of college students who at one time were alcoholics and drug users and held a Bible class for them at the British ambassador's residence once a week. When the ambassador left to make room for his replacement, the group lost its mentor and meeting place. The Russian pastor, who was the associate pastor of the English-speaking church we attended at Gorky Park, asked me if he could hold the class in our apartment, having had tea with us to get acquainted and seeing that we had plenty of room for a gathering. After checking with the Embassy if this was allowed, I agreed to have the class at our house on the condition that we all met at the Metro before going to our apartment and walked there together. I did not want young people coming and going at different times, especially since our building held other countries' Embassy personnel and had a guard (a woman) sitting at the entrance and monitoring all who came and went.

For a month, we met every Thursday with the pastor and his group at the Metro near our house, and all walked together to the building. After the pastor held his Bible session, I invited the youth to have tea and cookies, and got to know them and their way of life in the city. The group began to grow in size, as their friends bragged about the evenings, which they thoroughly enjoyed. Jerry and I thus came to be their advisors and confidants, even holding a few classes in marriage counseling and discussions about life in America at their request.

One evening, we received a phone call from a man who said he was a Chechen and a Bible believer who was in Moscow to get a visa for Germany. He asked to join our Thursday evening class, which he had seen advertised at the Gorky Park church area. My heart went to my feet, since I immediately thought that the Russian authorities must have put him up to it, knowing that they disliked having young people proselytized to any faith but Orthodoxy, Russia's accepted religion. The fact that this was a Chechen calling, make it all the worse. The Chechens, a group of dissidents and fighters from the Russian province of Chechnya, who later became outright terrorists, had been fiercely fighting for independence from Russia, and the Russians had been bombing their province unmercifully. A group of them living in Chechnya had come from Germany some time before and settled there, and the Germans were granting them visas as they became persecuted by the Russians. Since I felt I had no choice, I invited him to meet our group at the Metro.

The Chechen came to the Metro despite my hope that he would change his mind and we would not have to deal with him. He had a large duffle bag, which he was carrying as he stepped out of the Metro. I told him that I needed to inspect its contents for the safety of the people living in our building. He readily agreed and said "those are my life's belongings; it's all I possess." In fact, the bag contained his clothes and shaving gear, a Bible, and little else of consequence. I had some of the young people help him carry it to the house.

It was a lively Bible class that evening, with the Chechen describing how the Bible-believers had to hold their church in each other's homes in an underground fashion, while authorities prowled in their back yards to try to catch them in the act. They were forbidden to practice all but Orthodoxy. He explained that he had been at work when the Russians bombed his village, and his entire family was killed when a bomb hit their home. "I had no family left and nothing to live for," he said, "so I decided to see if I could get a visa for Germany and start life all over again." The man appeared to be in his late fifties. The young students listened attentively and asked many questions.

Once the Bible session finished and all had tea and cookies and left, I asked the Chechen if he had eaten supper. When he shook his head, I invited him to join Jerry and me, and we had an interesting conversation at the table. I liked the man and wanted to believe that he was who he said he was. Once we finished eating, I asked where he was staying while in Moscow, and he explained that the airport benches were his home. He lacked funds to get a hotel and was hoping to get his visa soon. After giving him some money for food, Jerry and I sent him on his way, hoping that we would have no repercussions from his visit.

The next evening, as I was preparing dinner, the doorbell rang. I went to the door, and peeking through the peep hole, stepped back in shock when I saw the hall filled with gun-toting militia men, aiming at our door. "Jerry!" I called in panic. "We have a hall full of visitors."

As Jerry stepped to the door and opened it cautiously, a man asked in English, "Jerry, are you and

Jennie okay? I'm the Embassy's RSO (safety officer), and we were told that you and Jennie were being held captive by the Chechens. The militia brought me here to help extricate you from them."

A man stepped in front of the RSO and said in Russian, "I'm the interpreter. Our understanding was that you were both visited by a group of Chechens last night, and they were holding you captive," he explained. "We're here to set you free."

"We are fine," Jerry insisted to both of them. "Please come inside and check for yourselves. There were no Chechens here last night, and we certainly were not being held captive by anyone. Please come see for yourself," Jerry motioned to the Russian, opening the door wide. The Russian KGB (we believed) officer strained his neck and looked past Jerry at me but refused to enter. "No, no," he insisted. "We will not cross the threshold if our help is not needed, but we want to warn you that the Chechens kidnap and kill at will. It is dangerous to associate with them." He turned his back on us, clicked his heels, and told the militia men to put their guns down. "There are no Chechens here," he said as he propelled them to the end of the hall and down the stairs to the entrance.

The RSO officer stayed to talk to us, surprised that this had been a false alarm, one that he had not ever been involved in before. He was relieved to learn that we were not in any danger and left soon, requesting that I prepare a report on the situation in the morning once I got to the Embassy. We breathed a sigh of relief, understanding fully that it would be dangerous for us to continue to allow the pastor to hold his Bible sessions in our apartment in the future. This proved to be true, as the Russians sent their Foreign Affairs officer to the Embassy to formally warn me that I was endangering the people in our building by harboring Chechens and if that continued, I would be asked to leave the country.

Chapter 34

German Trip Ends Dangerously

After we had lived more than a year in Moscow, our children decided that we were settled enough for them to come visit us, and our first grandchildren were old enough to travel. Both our son and daughter had new additions to their families; a daughter was born to our son, and a son was born to our daughter while we were away. I had flown back to the States to be with both my first grandchildren when they were born and was anxious to see them again.

Since our son and his wife had not been abroad, they decided to stop in Munich, Germany, to explore the city and invited us to fly there to join them. Jerry and I arranged for a driver to take us to Moscow's Sheremetyevo airport and asked him to pick us up when we returned to Moscow. We planned to return several days before our son and his wife arrived, so we could bring them to our Moscow apartment.

After several delightful days of exploring Munich and its surroundings, we took a taxi to the airport for our Aeroflot flight back to Moscow. The Russian plane was delayed for four hours in the German airport, and I called our Russian driver to tell him to pick us up at midnight, when the plane was scheduled to finally arrive there.

Exhausted after our long wait and the hassle of getting through customs, we looked for our driver at the Moscow Sheremetyevo airport. For some reason, he did not show up, so I went outside to search for a ride back to our apartment, hoping to find an honest-looking taxi driver who would not "rip us off" too extensively. I found a serious young Zhiguli (Fiat) driver who gave me a reasonable offer, and although his little Fiat-like car looked worn and small, I felt we had little choice if we wanted to get home before dawn. We squeezed ourselves and our luggage into the tiny automobile that had no seatbelts and proceeded in the dark of the night to ride home.

The road to and from the airport was divided by a central grassy median, and the dark pavement lacked any kind of electric lighting. The night was pitch black, but the road was filled with speeding vehicles to and from the airport, at least when we started out. It would take an hour to get into the city, and as we proceeded at a decent speed of about 50 mph, it became darker as we progressed and met less traffic. The young driver was a careful one and kept his Zhiguli at a fairly low speed, staying on the right side of the two-lane road. About ten miles from the airport, we saw a white van standing in the right lane of the highway, and the driver moved to the passing lane to get around it. As he did so, the driver of the van sped out of his lane directly in front of our car, and the Zhiguli was not able to stop quickly enough to avoid it. The crash sent us forward, with our legs cutting into the back bar of the front seats, but we were otherwise not plunged further than that. Our small car stopped in its tracks, with the front bashed in and steam coming out of the radiator.

At the impact, the van cut through the opening of the median of the four-lane highway and came to a stop on the opposite side of the road. The driver and his companion were obviously unhurt, and the driver came to our car to see what condition we were in. Shocked but unhurt, Jerry and I also stepped out of the car, as did the driver. The car obviously could not proceed and stood in the middle of the cross road, with steam continuing to emanate.

As Jerry and I stepped onto the median, our driver and the driver of the van began to argue, with the van driver speaking in a strong Arabic accent. We were in the dark until a police car pulled behind the smoking Zhiguli, and two hefty policemen went up to the arguing drivers to join in the discussion. One of the policemen motioned me to join them and started asking me what had happened. I told him what I knew, and surprisingly the two officers got back in their police car and drove away, leaving us in the dark again. They placed no lights on the road to warn oncoming traffic, as we expected them to do. I was still standing on the road as I heard Jerry shout to me to get back on the median. I quickly obeyed, and as I did so, I heard the sound of a speeding car coming up behind us.

The car apparently did not see the Zhiguli or the two drivers still arguing on the road. It hit the Zhiguli with full force as well as the driver of the van, who was standing closest to it. Both went flying forward, with the Fiat stopping 500 feet ahead, the driver of the van lying motionless on the ground, and our driver still on the road behind them, badly shaken. The passengers of the car which caused the second accident seemed unhurt, with their large sedan sporting a noticeable dent on the side. They examined the man lying on the ground, looked at the crushed Zhiguli now smoking profusely, and in a rush to leave, got back into their sedan and sped away in the dark.

I was close to hysterics and grabbed Jerry's hand for comfort. We all stood that way for about fifteen minutes, with everyone climbing on the median except for the victim lying on the road. We heard an ambulance coming toward us, followed by a police car with the same officers who had left us in the dark. They gave orders to the ambulance drivers to pick up the victim and put him on a stretcher whose metal legs gave way as they tried to lift him into their vehicle.

While they were struggling to get him into the ambulance, one of the officers stepped up to Jerry and me, asking us how we planned to get home. I told them I was an Embassy officer and needed to get to a telephone to call the Embassy driver to pick us up. They offered to take me to their police building not far from the accident. They motioned me to their car, and while Jerry stayed behind to get our luggage from the crumpled Zhiguli, I went with them to their headquarters.

Shaken by the incident, I was frightened as we drove for quite a distance on a dark, bumpy country road, and relieved when we came to a small lit-up building, where I was able to call the Embassy to send a driver to pick us up. The police gave me a ride back, warning me that I might be in trouble, since the government did not like foreigners to be involved in night-time accidents. Although I ignored their comments, which sent chills down my spine—for the first time, I became suspicious about the entire incident and wondered if it had been staged by the KGB. There were too many questionable occurrences—our reliable driver not showing up, a van standing on a busy highway, no lights placed behind the accident by the police, the same cops returning with an ambulance not knowing who, if anyone, was hurt, and a second car speeding in the dark and hitting a person, who could have been me had Jerry not warned me to get to the median. I shuddered at the thought and the suspicion that someone may be unhappy with my presence in Moscow and was relieved when we returned to where Jerry was waiting on the median with our suitcases by his side. He had begun to worry about my being gone so long and started to wonder if the policemen had been legitimate.

It was a relief to see our Embassy driver pull up a half hour later, and when he started speeding down the road, we both asked him to slow down slightly so we could get home safely, still shaken by the whole affair.

Despite a disastrous start—I was relieved that our children were not with us during the accident—we were able to pick up our son and his family two days later, enjoying the chance to show them the better side of Moscow.

Two weeks later, the driver of the Zhiguli called me and asked me to talk to a judge and explain to him what had happened that night. He said the police claimed he was at fault, and he desperately needed my support to extricate himself from a bad situation. I was happy to oblige.

Chapter 35

Return to Latvia Fifty Years Later

T he stay in Moscow made it easier for me to travel
to the Baltic country of Latvia, where I was born
more than fifty years earlier. I was able to get from my
mother the telephone number of one of my cousins who
still lived there, Aunt Manya's daughter. My aunt, who
had been sent to Siberia with her three children after
her husband was killed by the communists, survived the
ordeal and was miraculously able to get in touch with
my father during Khrushchev's thaw.

As she later told Dad in a letter, the four — my Aunt
Manya, her fourteen-year-old son, an eight-year-old
daughter, and a young baby of eighteen months — were
dumped in a town called Krasnoyarsk, at that time a
closed city from which people were not allowed to
leave because of its nuclear facilities. The authorities
dropped them off in a small hut at the edge of town.
Aunt Manya said they would have starved except for
the kind people living around her who left food on

their doorstep, wrapped in scarves or small tablecloths. Manya, who came from an educated family and was a school teacher by profession, was forced to chop wood and milk cows for the survival of her family.

She eventually found a job as a factory worker, and was able to ask a kind, high-level communist employer who respected and admired her to put an ad in a New York paper printed in Russian, to which my dad subscribed. The ad sought Aunt Manya's brothers and provided an address to correspond with her.

Dad happened to notice the ad and could not believe his eyes when he realized that it was from his sister. In responding to it, he got in touch with his missing sister whom he saw last in 1944 in a train in Latvia as she was being deported to Siberia. In her letter, she explained her current situation—her oldest son was a physicist, her oldest daughter a schoolteacher, and her youngest was studying medicine. When asked, she told Dad that they wanted to return to Latvia. Her oldest daughter had a possibility to teach in Riga where there was an opening, but they could not afford the trip there from Siberia.

Dad could not send them money, which would never reach its destination, but he found a store in Buffalo, New York, that was able to send packages of goods to Siberia bought from the store. It entailed paying 100 percent duty on the goods, which consisted of fine materials, expensive leather shoes and jackets, and other costly items. Every payday after discovering it, Dad sent Aunt Manya a package with goods she was able to sell and earn enough money to buy tickets to get the family to Latvia, that is, all but the oldest married son, the physicist who was not allowed to leave Krasnoyarsk, given his profession. Ironically enough, they were able to find housing in the same part of town where they once lived, in a house they rented to their former employees.

Aunt Manya died before I could see her, but Dad continued to be in touch with her oldest daughter, my cousin Lydiya, the school teacher, and even had a telephone number for her, which Mom gave me. I was able to use it to get in touch with her daughter, my niece. Lydiya had married and moved to Daugavpils, but her two children were living in Riga. My youngest cousin Olga was also nearby in Daugava, by the shore.

They were surprised but pleased to receive my call, telling them that I now lived in Moscow and would be coming to Riga for a visit. I said I wanted to introduce them to my husband, who was traveling with me. My niece Katya and her brother Sergey came to see us first in our hotel in Riga. They were not sure how well I could speak Russian, but the two young people had some knowledge of English, having learned it in school, so they were sent to greet us. Both were pleased when Jerry and I were able to converse freely in Russian.

Katya and Sergey took us to meet with Aunt
Manya's youngest daughter Olga and her husband, who
lived in Daugava, a place well known for its beautiful
beaches and shore life. Many Russians traveled there
for summer vacations before the Soviet Union fell apart,
and it was still part of the commonwealth, but the dis-
solution of the Soviet empire made it more difficult for
Russian travelers, especially since the Latvians were
not too fond of the Russians, who invaded their country
during the war and sent many of their own soldiers to
live there. The soldiers and their families retired to the
area in droves.

Native Latvians became a minority right after the
war, as Russians took advantage of the benefits the Baltic
country had to offer, and literally made the natives sec-
ond-class citizens. As Latvia gained its independence
when the Soviet Union fell apart, the Latvian natives
reversed this, making it difficult for the Russians to live
comfortably in Latvia by passing strict citizenship laws,
such as a requirement to know Latvian—hard for many
to learn since it was so different from Russian—and a
refusal to allow noncitizens to own property.

I asked my niece how the country treated them, and
she pointed out that there was a grandfather clause for
those Russians—like my family—who were living in
the country prior to the Russian invasion. My family
also spoke fluent Latvian, which they had learned from

231

their parents, who knew it when Latvia was still an independent country.

"My poor husband is not as lucky," my niece Katya told me. "He is a son of retired Russian military and speaks only Russian. He says he doesn't know what country he belongs to and is frustrated that I can buy property—such as the apartment we now live in—with his money, but he is not allowed to do so, since he has not passed the citizenship requirements."

Olga was delighted to meet us, introducing her handsome husband to us. Vova shook my hand, then gave me a big hug, and explained to my husband that we had been childhood friends as we were growing up in Latvia. "We even thought we were drowning once while swimming in the Daugava Lake, while the water was only up to our knees. I still remember Zhenya yelling, "Save us" to a gentleman nearby, who pulled us both out of the water laughing," he reminisced.

Vova was an only child of wealthy parents, and I remember how my brother and I used to send him home shortly after he arrived, preferring to play alone together. What a delight it was to meet him now and find out he had married my cousin. Vova showed us many photographs from their family album, among them ones of my parents at their wedding.

The day after our arrival, Vova took us to tour downtown Riga, a beautiful town with lovely old houses and brick streets. As we walked, Vova pointed to a large apartment building, with a smaller home in front of it. "That building, as well as the twelve-room house in front of it," said Vova, "once belonged to my parents and I have the paperwork to claim it tomorrow. I haven't done that because the building is in disrepair and would require a bundle of money to clean it up. The house, however, is also mine, and I plan to claim it as soon as possible. The paperwork on it is already at City Hall."

"How does that work?" I asked him. "Do the people who live there now just move out of it?"

"That's the rub," he responded sadly. "They have up to a year to find another place to live, and we will just have to wait until they do. The house we live in now and have put a lot of money into to renovate is also being sought by the people who once owned it, so we have to find a place to live until we can move into this one."

I later learned that Vova and my cousin had to vacate their current house long before they could acquire the large one he showed us. They moved into a small hut-like place, unhappy with it and probably with us because we had not offered to provide money for them to renovate the large apartment building and claim it as their own. To them, anyone coming from American had money to spare and would not have a problem financing at least half a million dollars, so relatives could reclaim their property. The thought made me very sad and aware of the misconceptions held by my relatives of our own middle-class existence in which we both had to work to keep up with our mortgage, college payments, and bills that ate up a budget.

My oldest cousin Lydiya had moved to Daugavpils, a small town on the Polish border which housed many Russians and where I was born and lived until my dad acquired a job in Riga. I was anxious to visit Lydiya and her husband, to relive memories of childhood, and to visit the graves of my grandparents and other relatives. Daugavpils was dear to my heart, and I wanted to see it while there was a chance to visit and before we returned to the States. I rented a van and a driver, and my young cousins took Jerry and me to visit their mother in Daugavpils.

As we approached the small town, a lovely lake greeted us, a lake I remembered swimming in as a child. As we drove beside it, I smelled the swampy aroma of surrounding verdure and felt like it was very familiar and dear to me. I recalled skating on the lake as a child, when the cold Baltic winters froze it from end to end, and riding in a sleigh with prancing horses as we glided over its smooth surface. There was something déjà vu about it all, and I almost choked on the tears that welled up in my eyes and caught in my throat.

The visit with my cousin Lydiya and her husband was memorable. She introduced me to their pastor as she showed me the church where Dad practically grew up, and when I told the pastor that we still sang the Old

Orthodox liturgy in a mall church in New Jersey, he decided to test me by asking me to sing a familiar song in a certain melody (there were eight melodies altogether). Not able to recall the particular one he wanted, I sang the song as I remembered it.

"That was the first, not the third melody" he joyfully teased me when I explained that I was not that familiar with how to start the melodies and, in the past, followed my Dad's lead, "but I can see that you still remember the ancient singing, which pleases me no end." He took us to the cemetery where my grandparents were buried, and we paid our respects to their graves and the graves of aunts and uncles who all died during the war or soon thereafter.

My cousin Lydiya also got in touch with my mother's living relatives to let them know of my visit, and they were all anxious to meet with us. My mom had been nervous about us meeting her relatives, still cautious about the harm that could come to them from being related to an American working for the US government, and was hesitant to give me names and addresses, most of which she no longer had. She had no opportunity to keep in touch with her end of the family and learned about them only from Aunt Manya's letters.

I was extremely anxious to meet them as well and wanted to find out about my maternal grandmother and how she managed after we left Latvia. I was also trying to find out what my grandfather's last name was and if they heard about his fate—the general who left my grandmother to fight with the White Russian army against the communists. I soon learned in questioning my relatives that they either knew nothing of him or did not want to even talk about his past existence. Apparently, his name still engendered fear in my relatives, and no one could even tell me what his last name had been. One cousin said he died in the war, and that was all I could glean from them.

Aside from that, the visit went well, and they questioned me about my mom—how was she doing in America, did she speak and understand English, and was she happy? I left my mom's relatives feeling sad that she could not be there to give them hugs and reminisce about old times. Wars have a way of separating families forever.

Before we left Riga, my cousins took me to the location where our large stately brick house had stood before the Communists burned it down. In its place was a sandy and rocky hill, cluttered in its surroundings with refuse that people threw out on their way past it. A round sidewalk was barely visible nearby, with what looked like parts of a statue, broken asphalt-like rocks, formless and cluttering the sidewalk. I sighed as I remembered the lovely home that housed us in years gone by and said farewell to the past, looking forward to getting back to our two-story house in Virginia that still held a promise of happiness that was surely to come. God had taken me a long way from Latvia and had given me the chance to return to what was no longer my place in the sun.

Chapter 36

By the Grace of God

We returned from Moscow in 1997 and I was eventually able to return to the CIA, where I felt I belonged. I continued to work there until retirement, spending many fruitful years at the Agency. Jerry retired soon after our return from Moscow and started another career when he registered for a master's degree in divinity with Regent University in Virginia Beach, Virginia. Although he was able to take on-line courses until my retirement, he announced shortly thereafter that it was necessary for him to be physically on campus to complete courses for his degree, necessitating our move to Virginia Beach. I was reluctant to leave our Herndon home and the Washington, D.C. area, where I had been offered a consulting position to teach seminars on critical thinking and analytical writing to a number of federal agencies.

For eight years thereafter, I shuttled back and forth between Virginia Beach and D.C., staying for a week at a time in motels. The drive home was always a nightmare, with traffic standing for miles—the infamous rush hours which I always managed to catch. Despite the inconvenience of my travel, we thoroughly enjoyed the Virginia Beach area and I was happy with my training responsibilities. Jerry basked in his studies and developed a huge library to match his Slavic one, barely able to contain all his books in our modest house.

Four years after our move, we discovered to our dismay that Jerry had Parkinson's disease, brought on in large part by his year spent in Viet Nam under Agent Orange. He began to experience difficulties with his balance in 2009, pitching forward as he walked, and initially we thought that it was the result of having had surgery on both hips. It wasn't until he lost his balance completely while walking our dog and fell to the ground, refusing help from by-standers who wanted to call 911, that we realized something more formidable was at play. He stubbornly lifted himself with the help of a street sign to lean on and failed to tell me about his fall until he could no longer hide his condition. Other symptoms, primarily with his memory and writing, followed, and by 2014, when he could no longer handle his studies, we returned to our Herndon home, which I had insisted on renting when we left for Virginia Beach. I wanted to be closer to family and loyal neighbors whom I could call on in emergencies and I hoped for better medical care for him in the D.C.

area. My consulting business had shifted to traveling to different parts of the country to provide seminars, and I took Jerry with me on these trips.

Jerry's Parkinson's disease brought us closer to our family, and we basked in the love of our children and six grandchildren, who came to visit us in Virginia Beach and in Herndon. Our son and his family—two sons and a daughter—live in Atlanta, while our daughter, with her husband and three sons, made their home in Connecticut. We cherished our holidays with them and a 50th Wedding Anniversary celebration at our daughter's, surrounded by relatives.

We also developed a close friendship with a Russian family that had lived in our Herndon neighborhood for many years when Jerry stumbled on them while walking our dog and heard them speaking Russian. Jerry struck up a conversation, and from then on, they became our dearest friends. I partnered with the husband in teaching a graduate course for his thesis students, at his initiative, and his wife helped me with Jerry as one of his aides. These friends provided invaluable support when things fell apart in my life with Jerry's illness.

As his illness progressed, I tried to take care of Jerry at home in Herndon with the help of aides, but after his third bout with pneumonia, when he was hospitalized for a week and could no longer swallow on his own and required feeding directly through his stomach, I had to put him into a nursing home. We continued to see each other daily, although the home was in Arlington, a distance from our house. He would sit in the hallway near his room, pretending to read a paper, while watching for me to come in the afternoon, carrying his laundry or papers and books for him.

I enjoyed wheeling Jerry around the building and outside in good weather, and we spent many peaceful moments watching TV together and communicating silently. One day, as we listened to an evangelist on a religious network who said that God would never leave us or forsake us, Jerry burst into tears, surprising me. I had been wondering if his love for the Lord was still there, given the confused state of his mind, and this outburst convinced me that it had never left him. That outburst strengthened my own faith and gave me courage to face his death.

His death came in a hospital in Arlington, Virginia on February 6, 2017. Jerry seemed to have lost consciousness a day before his death and kept his eyes closed, his body still trying to catch a breath to survive. Nick left late into the night and Chris and I settled down on a window couch by his bed, when Chris unexpectedly got up and walked to his bedside. "Mom," she called quietly. "Dad's eyes are open."

I jumped to his side and his eyes turned to me, looking squarely into mine. I waved to make sure he saw me, and he blinked, but continued to look at me intently, as if trying to tell me something. It lasted only for a long moment, but a silent message passed between us before he closed his eyes and was gone.

Losing him was a heartache, but I believed that he would always remain a part of me, and it calmed me considerably. Later, while shopping in a store, I found a plaque that I have to this day. Its author is unknown, but the words still comfort me: *"Death leaves a heart-ache no one can heal ... love leaves a memory no one can steal."*

Several weeks after Jerry's death and his burial in New Jersey in the Old Orthodox cemetery next to my brother, I was back in Herndon and slowly began to get used to life without him. The little puppy that my sister had insisted I get after my twelve-year-old Schnoodle died of a heart condition while Jerry lay in a hospital with pneumonia was a welcome companion.

Toby was an entertaining little white ball of fur who loved to run after tennis balls. He had left a ball at the top of our stairway, which I neglected to see, and as I hurried to take out a garbage bag, I stepped on the ball and went flying to the bottom of a seven-step staircase, grabbing a railing on the left wall on my way down. I sat there for a while, telling Toby that I hurt my leg and he was at fault, then hopped outside to the garbage can and deposited the garbage bag. Excruciating pain hit me as I tried to get back in the house, and I crawled up the staircase, trying to keep my left leg from scraping it. I hopped to our living room couch and passed out from the pain.

My daughter Chris woke me up with her call to check on me. Dazed, I told her that I had just fallen down the stairs and hurt my left leg. "Mom," she exclaimed, "Is there anyone you can call to have it checked? You may have broken a bone."

"I'll call my dear neighbor Mary," I reassured her, "so don't worry. Call me later tonight."

After checking my leg, Mary discovered a very swollen ankle. She took me to the Emergency Room, where the X-rays indicated I had broken three major bones in my left leg, as well as two toes.

It took two months and eight pins to hold the bones together and to help them heal, as well as to get me out of a wheelchair so I could walk with a cane. I had to teach my final graduate class in a wheelchair. My sister Olga came immediately from New Jersey to take care of me, and after a week, my daughter-in-law replaced her. Once I had the surgery, Chris took me to her home in Connecticut to help finish the healing process.

The accident and my successful healing prompted me to question what the Lord wanted me to do with the rest of my life. I was seventy-eight years old but still feeling young at heart. I had given up my consulting when Jerry became too ill to travel. The dormant time in the wheelchair helped me to add to my memoir, but something was still missing in my life. I did not know what the Lord had in store for me and wondered how to best serve Him.

In looking at my options, I realized that the stairway would continue to be a challenge, but I was not prepared to live with either of my children. I began to pray for guidance and realized that I did not have to stay in place in Herndon. Jerry's inheritance from his parents of their home and property in Utah, which we used to visit family, was available. With Jerry gone, I could not picture myself spending a lot of time there without him. It seemed like a good time to put the property up for sale, and I put it on the market. God blessed me with a good buyer, and I sold the property quickly and advantageously.

I yearned to be closer to the cemetery where Jerry was buried in Millville and searched for a vacation home in the Atlantic City area, less than thirty minutes away. I reasoned that a shore home there would be an advantage for the rest of the family as well, and it satisfied my desire to be near the shore. With the inflated prices in the New Jersey beach areas, however, I could not find anything appropriate. My friends advised me to look at the Delaware beaches where they had spent many enjoyable summers.

In my first Internet search for Delaware shore houses, I stumbled on a lovely home that seemed to meet my criteria for comfort and safety. I visited the Delaware beach area and looked at a number of lovely living arrangements, but when I walked into the house I saw on the Internet, there was something that unmistakably drew me to it. I knew I could be comfortable there, even alone. With reluctant approval from my loved ones who were concerned that I knew no one in the area, I put a deposit on the house and finalized the sale.

While looking at Delaware properties, I also spotted a church that attracted me, and as soon as I attended its first Sunday service, I knew that the Lord had brought me to this area for a good reason. The pastor was inspiring, and its members were loving and friendly, making me feel comfortable in their presence.

When I think back about the events since Jerry's death, I realize that my fall down the stairs was a blessing in disguise. It provided me with having family around for another two months, and it kept me from concentrating on Jerry's passing; it forced me to focus on my healing and recovery rather than on Jerry's absence. And, most importantly, it was in large part responsible for my decision to leave the comfort of the Herndon area and strike out on my own.

I moved to Delaware in late August, six months after Jerry's death, and have been happy here ever since. The love and fellowship I have experienced as a member of the church has far exceeded my expectations, and I'm blessed with neighbors equally friendly and caring. I feel close to my Savior as I study his

Word and try to follow his teaching. I am genuinely blessed with a peace that surpasses all understanding, and I believe that Jerry is smiling at me from above.

THE END

CPSIA information can be obtained
at www.ICGtesting.com
Printed in the USA
FFHW011436170419
51843336-57228FF